T
GOLDEN
GIRLS

THE GOLDEN GIRLS
THEME SONG

"Thank You For Being A Friend"

Thank you for being a friend.
Travelled down the road and back again.
Your heart is true,
You're a real pal and a confidant.
And if you threw a party,
Invited everyone you knew,
You would see
The biggest gift would be from me,
And the card attached would say,
Thank you for being a friend.

THE GOLDEN GIRLS

Created by: SUSAN HARRIS

With an introduction and
commentary by John Marriott

BOXTREE

First published in 1991
by BOXTREE LIMITED, 36 Tavistock Street,
London WC2E 7PB

10 9 8 7 6 5 4 3 2 1

1 85283 676 8

Printed and bound in Great Britain by Cox & Wyman, Reading, Berkshire

A catalogue record for this book is available from the British Library.

CONTENTS

· *Introduction* ·

Television, like car factories and vineyards, seems to embrace short periods of time when it places mediocrity on the back burner and gives birth to a stream of classic products. In America, the exhilarating era of live television comedy, during which Mel Brooks, Carl Reiner and Woody Allen cut their teeth as gag-writers, produced the Sid Caesar Show, while in Britain the Sixties were prime time for Tony Hancock, Eric Sykes and Warren Mitchell.

A recent crop of excellent comedies (see *Yes Minister* and *Fawlty Towers* for further details) highlight the threadbare nature of others. Under-developed characters walk self-consciously into a drab sitting room to announce unfunny lines, while the 'audience' hoots artificially on the soundtrack.

Just when it seemed that scriptwriters were all giggling twelve year-olds scribbling in the playground between classes, along came *The Golden Girls* in 1985 like a supercharged express train. Created by Susan Harris, who was also responsible for *Soap* and *Benson*, it gave off an exhilarating breeze in its wake and woke up a vast TV audience from its prolonged sofa-slumber.

Armed with an arsenal of biting one-liners which are let off with crackerjack efficiency, the series also stood American TV comedy on its head. Mercifully free of the sentimental goo in which comic actors often drown, it also elbowed the notion that key players have to be perfectly manicured young things who have spent more time in front of the mirror than in learning lines and who might be more suited to the front cover of Vogue.

Most sitcoms exist in a happy family vacuum. Even after squabbles, illness and death, the family pulls together by the end of the programme and re-affirms cosy family values. Not so *The Golden Girls*. Certain critics and industry figures sneered in advance and claimed loudly that a comedy about four unattached, ageing women (divorcees and widows among them) would drive itself to the edge of the cliff and then quickly fall off.

Instead the series has been a smash the world over. Tired of a bland diet in which anaemic comedies and TV commercials are joined invisibly at the seams, viewers have latched on to the funny, tough and sometimes moving experiences of these four single women who share a house in Miami Beach and refuse to become dozy Florida pensioners. In a location which is paradise for many, they battle with age, death, men and cholesterol. Yet even situations which are fraught or harrowing are always pierced by machine-gun humour and spicy wit.

The last series was ushered in with an emphasis on tough realism. Dorothy (Bea Arthur), normally tall, strident and healthy, falls victim to a mystery illness and becomes quickly convinced that she is going to die of cancer or some other dreadful illness. Weak, listless and with all her punchy vigour drained out of her, she climbs into bed and stays there. Putting her life in order, and deciding which possessions go to which of her three friends, she is surprised to learn from the doctor that she has no physical ailment but may well be subconsciously distraught about old age, dying or not being in love.

Such high-octane drama seems a planet removed from the stuff of comedy. Yet, while Dorothy bemoans her fate and seems destined for death, many funny lines dance their way across the script. Nymphomaniac Blanche (Rue McClanahan), for whom thoughts of sex happen more rapidly than breathing, suggests that Dorothy's problem may be that she has been starved of sex for some time.

Dorothy's feisty mother Sophia (Estelle Getty) fires off a typically razor-sharp response: "Maybe it works – you're as healthy as a horse!"

As *The Golden Girls* moved away from straight comedy to issues-based episodes which still left room for laughter, artificial insemination was the next touchy topic to be covered during peak viewing time. Blanche's unmarried daughter arrives in Florida to consult a fertility specialist about artificial insemination. Her man-hungry mother, who equates insemination with bouts of lust and night-time frolics, just cannot comprehend at first and, in her frivolous, self-regarding way, stutters:

"What does one wear to the sperm bank?" "Something attractive in rubber," snaps Dorothy.

Dorothy (Bea Arthur) is the sensible backbone of the friendly foursome. With a deep boom which exudes an air of authority, she orders the lives of her three companions (a flirt, an airhead and a crusty old demon) with a deliberate, slow-moving manner which is the very voice of common sense. A divorced schoolteacher to boot, she knows how to deflate a situation with warmth yet puncture infant behaviour with sardonic wit. Tall, gangly and relaxed, she drapes herself over a sofa with ease.

However, in reality, Bea Arthur is tremendously shy. While on screen she is given to bossing her chums around in a forthright manner, she can be awkward and self-conscious in public.

"My problem is my size," she confesses. "People expect me to be in charge because I am so tall. I look the part. On stage I'm absolutely omnipotent but really I'm neurotically shy."

With stage credits which include Woody Allen's *The Floating Lightbulb*, *Fiddler On The Roof*, *The Threepenny Opera* and *Mame* (for which she won a Tony award), Bea has also starred in a number of films including *Lovers And Other Strangers*, *That Kind Of Woman* and *Mame* again.

Her hit television series, *Maude*, was later followed by

Amanda (inspired by the lunacy of *Fawlty Towers*) after which Bea took a much-needed break to tend to her sick mother. It was during this worrying time that she was offered the part of Dorothy, a character which has since brought her an Emmy award.

A peppy 64, and, like Dorothy, divorced, Bea is a diehard New Yorker who returns as often as possible from her home in Brentwood, California, primarily for a quick theatre fix. A keen charity worker and mother of two sons, she seems contented and centred despite the handwringing experience of a husband (director Gene Saks) who fled the family nest for a younger woman after 29 years of marriage. Probably far from her thoughts at the time, the experience did, however, prepare her substantially for the psychology of *The Golden Girls*.

Dorothy's mother Sophia is wonderfully fleshed out by stage veteran Estelle Getty. Given to wisecracking that she's played mother to everyone except Atilla the Hun, she loads the role of Sophia with fire, brimstone and a nonstop flow of witty one-liners and cracking put-downs. By far the most severe of the four characters, she fixes her partners with a beady eye and tight lips, while letting sparks fly from under her abundant mop of grey curls. A Sicilian who has survived frugal times and hard knocks, Sophia is possessed of a cynical bite which can chew on others' foibles and cause viewers to convulse.

Yet even Sophia herself can be stamped on by the dopey Rose. Sophia moans:

"My arthritis is bothering me, my social security cheque is late and I realised I haven't showered with a man for 22 years."

"Ma, pop's been dead 27 years," corrects Dorothy.

"What's your point?" snaps Sophia.

"Isn't it obvious," chimes Rose. "She showered with a dead man for 5 years."

As Getty herself, explains, "I know this lady I'm playing. She's partly me and partly my imagination, but she's an original and that's what I've been playing all my life, original characters."

Her success in playing a wide range of mothers included her award-winning role as Mrs Berkoff in the Broadway production of *Torch Song Trilogy*, as well as Cher's mum in *Mask* and Barry Manilow's in *Copacabana*. With both Golden Globe and Emmy for her performance as Sophia, she has convinced the world that she is older than she is. Sophia is 85, Estelle 65.

After fifty years in the business, Sophia transformed Estelle into an overnight success. Married with two sons, she looks trim and youthful in sneakers and blue jeans, while her continuous pep has enabled her to speak out on behalf of senior citizens and AIDS charities, while somehow finding time to write a book, *"If I Knew Then What I Know Now – So What?"*.

The tranquil, rural surroundings of Rue McClanahan's California home, which includes a botanical garden with storybook paths, give no clue as to the presence of Blanche, the lusty Southern belle she plays in *The Golden Girls*.

With a bust which enters the room several seconds before she does, and with the body-hugging togs more favoured by teenagers, she is the shrill voice of sex which reminds her three housemates of their own womanly needs. The widowed owner of the house in Miami Beach where they all live, Blanche is so vain that she seems to spend much time in preening herself after getting out of bed but before stepping into the kitchen in her dressing gown. A self-styled broad who knows how to turn men into feverish schoolboys, she also reveals a healthy streak of decency, compassion, generosity and even vulnerability.

Rue's Broadway appearance in *Father's Day*, her role as Vivian Cavander Harmon in *Maude* and countless contributions to *Lou Grant*, *The Love Boat* et al, served her well until the advent of *The Golden Girls*, in which she was first cast as the simpering Rose.

"The part of Rose was ninety percent mine. But I'd

played that role before, I wanted to be Blanche. I knew immediately how to play her, the attitude, body language, her mannerisms and accent. I connected with her straight away. I wanted it so badly."

Her conversation is laced with references to a rollercoaster life of five marriages and as many divorces, a survival test which has enabled Rue to convince viewers as the man-conscious Blanche. Her global popularity has enabled her to start up her own television production company and launch a line of clothing, called, aptly, *Very Rue*.

She inhabits a quite different planet from Rose (Betty White), the naive, slow-thinking widow who views life as a romantic musical. A sweet innocent on whom reality has left no scars, she gawps uncomprehendingly at her friends, perplexed by Sophia's sardonic wit, Dorothy's common sense and Blanche's over-ripe libido. Never simply a victim of others' intelligence, she is also able to exert control over her fellow females.

Forty years of television, as well as five Emmys for her efforts, have made Betty White one of the best known faces on American TV. *Life With Elizabeth*, *The Mary Tyler Moore Show*, the quiz show *Just Men* (which she hosted) are among her popular triumphs. A committed animal lover, she has been honoured many times for her dedication to animal care and welfare, while her first book, *Betty White's Pet Love*, discusses the therapeutic benefit of animals on humans.

The credibility of the characters and the clout of the series has already attracted guest stars who include Bob Hope, Mickey Rooney and Burt Reynolds.

Each week the four ladies offer up a charismatic blend of exuberance, honesty and wit, while also homing in on some difficult issues and, in so doing, touch the lives of all kinds of people. Even the Queen Mother, whom you may think prefers to be shielded from the glass-strewn avenues of real life, insisted that the foursome appear at The Royal Variety Performance at the London Palladium.

JOHN MARRIOTT

JOB HUNTING

Written by:
KATHY SPEER & TERRY GROSSMAN
Directed by: PAUL BOGART

· Introduction ·

JOB HUNTING is a shining example of how *The Golden Girls'* penchant for fast-lane dialogue and punchy wit never squashes the heavyweight issues which usually provide the ballast of each episode.

Writers Kathy Speer and Terry Grossman here home in on the problems of job redundancy in late middle-age. Rose, the simpering innocent of the team, has been laid off from the grief counselling centre where she has worked for years. Fretting about her sudden loss of purpose, and emphasizing encroaching mortality to boot (a running theme throughout *The Golden Girls*), she declares mournfully to Dorothy:

"You can't help me find a job. Nobody or nothing can make me young again."

In the wee small hours, which stress her lonely anxiety all the more, Rose, all downturned lip and hunched shoulders, embraces the plight of many:

"I have tried. I just haven't told you. I've had dozens of job interviews since the Centre closed. No one wants me. I need something to do with my life. I never think of myself as old but every one else does. Maybe I am old. Old and useless . . .and terrified."

In a speech which is central to the entire episode, and is a rare event in primetime comedy, Rose is anxious, miserable, desperate yet determined.

However, the build-up to the central passage is completely frivolous. By unfolding proceedings through the comic banter between Blanche and Sophia (the figure-fussy

Blanche wants raw vegetables, Sophia, the diehard Sicilian, prefers pepperoni), Speer and Grossman intentionally overshadow the fads of the diet-obsessed millions with the serious issue to come. The free-wheeling exchange and loopy non-sequiturs, essential to any *Golden Girls'* episode, only give much more clout to questions of redundancy when they arise. Blanche's insistence that she once had a Scarlett O'Hara-style, 18" waistline, as well as Sophia's sarcastic jabs, are the heart of the comic routine. Revealing her natural intransigence, Sophia declares that anything but pepperoni will cause her to emit unthinkable odours throughout the house.

An episode which appears as simply a fast-moving conveyor-belt of smart jokes is typically loaded with much more. The tendency of many women to eat their way through worry is drawn in by means of a comic binge on cookies and cheesecake. This is immediately followed by another peek at mortality when Dorothy looks back to Barry Glick, a man she hero-worshipped as an eager teenager.

This next gives way to a vigorous conversation between the four friends about their first experience of sex, during which jokey references to inadequate men and decent orgasms are thick on the ground.

Rose: "Being near Charlie was always nice, but it was five years before I knew what made your eyes go back in your head. Dorothy, did you have . . . uh . . . ?"

Dorothy: "How could I? I mean it always seemed to happen before I was in the room."

CAST
DOROTHY, ROSE, BLANCHE, SOPHIA, MILTON.

ACT ONE
Scene 1

KITCHEN – EARLY EVENING

(Blanche, singing 'Sleep Kentucky Baby', prepares a raw vegetable platter. Sophia enters, crosses to refrigerator, opens it, stares inside)

BLANCHE   "Skeeters am a hummin' on the
Honeysuckle vine
Sleep Kentucky Babe
Sandman am a-comin' to this little
Babe o'mine
Sleep Kentucky Babe
Silver moon am shinin' in the
Heavens up above
Bobolink am pinin' for his little
Lady love
You is mighty lucky
Babe of old Kentucky
Close your eyes and sleep
Fly away
Fly away fly away babe
Fly away and rest."

SOPHIA   We're out of pepperoni. I'm starving, and we're out of pepperoni.

BLANCHE   I'm sorry, Sophia. Honey, would you like some celery stuffed with cottage cheese?

SOPHIA   I can't eat cottage cheese. It repeats on me.
(Dorothy enters)

DOROTHY	Hello, Hello. Hi, Blanche. How are you sweet mother? *(Kisses Sophia)*
SOPHIA	We're out of pepperoni.
DOROTHY	Did you call Dan Rather?
SOPHIA	I'm starving.
DOROTHY	I defrosted some chicken. We'll eat in half an hour.
SOPHIA	I can't eat chicken. It repeats on me.
DOROTHY	Look, Ma, you don't have to make excuses. If you don't want chicken, just say, 'I don't want chicken'.
SOPHIA	I don't want chicken.
DOROTHY	Good.
SOPHIA	It repeats on me. I want pepperoni.
DOROTHY	Blanche, Blanche, would you like some broiled chicken?
BLANCHE	Oh, no, thank you. I'm having a raw vegetable plate. You probably haven't noticed it, but I've put on three pounds.
SOPHIA	On each side.
BLANCHE	I used to have a waist just like Scarlett O'Hara. Well, you know, that girl had an eighteen inch waistline.
DOROTHY	Blanche, that girl – and her waistline – were fiction. *(Rose enters, distraught)*
ROSE	It's terrible. Just terrible. I am so upset.
DOROTHY	Rose, honey, sit down. Sweetheart, tell us all about it. Ma, would you get Rose some water?
SOPHIA	*(Sophia rises and walks around kitchen table)*

What is she going to do with water? Has water ever made *you* feel better when *you* were upset? Have you ever heard anyone say, 'Thank God, the water's here!'? Call me when dinner is ready.
(*Sophia exits*)

ROSE   I'm fine. Don't worry about me. It's all those other people . . .

BLANCHE Was it some kind of accident? No, don't tell me. If I get upset I'll eat.

DOROTHY What happened, Rose?

ROSE   They closed the Centre.

BLANCHE Not your grief counselling centre?

DOROTHY No, Blanche. The Kennedy Space Centre. She wanted to be the first Lutheran on the moon.

BLANCHE Oh, Rose. You're out of a job.

ROSE   Well, I can't worry about that now.

DOROTHY Well, sure you can, honey. I'll help you. Food, clothing, shelter . . .

ROSE   Oh, come on. It's not that serious.

DOROTHY Yes it could be. Rose, you and I are in the same boat. If we miss a couple of paychecks we are in big trouble.

BLANCHE Thank God I had the foresight to marry money.
(*Dorothy slaps Blanche's hand*)

DOROTHY Tramp.

ROSE   Dorothy, my main concern is making sure those miserable people find other sources of help. Then I'll get a job. I'm dependable, friendly, loyal, eager . . .

DOROTHY That's great. If she learns to catch a frisbee in her teeth, she can get work as a golden retriever.

ACT ONE
Scene 2

LANAI – SEVERAL DAYS LATER

(Milton, sits on a chaise lounge chair alone, reading Newsweek. Dorothy enters, and sits. She stares at Milton)

DOROTHY	*(A beat)* Hello.
MILTON	Hello. *(Milton returns to his reading)*
DOROTHY	*(After a beat)* I'm Dorothy.
MILTON	Milton.
DOROTHY	Pleased to meet you, Milton.
MILTON	Likewise. *(He returns to reading)*
DOROTHY	I live here.
MILTON	Oh.
DOROTHY	You don't.
MILTON	I live over on Dorado.
DOROTHY	Oh. Uh-huh.
MILTON	It's about a twenty minute walk. But I usually take the bus.
DOROTHY	Are you waiting for one now?
MILTON	No. I'm learning to get in touch with my emotions.
DOROTHY	Tell me, will it take long? You know, you're reading my Newsweek.
MILTON	Oh I'm sorry. *(Rose enters)*
ROSE	Oh, Dorothy. I see you've met Milton.

DOROTHY   Yes, we were just getting acquainted.
          (*Then sotto*)
          Dump him, Rose. He's driftwood.

ROSE   What?
          (*Realising*)
          Oh, no, Dorothy. Milton's from the Centre.
          His partner ran off with his wife and all the
          money from the business.

DOROTHY   Oh, Milton, I'm sorry. Keep the Newsweek.

ROSE   (*Takes Milton by the arm and walks him into the
          house*) Now, here's the address of a private
          counselling service and in the meantime, my
          number's down there here at the bottom. Now
          don't hesitate to call, any time, day or night.

DOROTHY   Day or night?
          (*She follows to living room*)

MILTON   Thanks again Rose.

ROSE   Oh, you're welcome, Milton. Now you let me
          know how it works out.

MILTON   I certainly will.

ROSE   No more tears.
          (*They ad-lib goodbyes. Milton exits. Rose sighs*)
          He's such a royal pain in the butt. But it's part
          of my job.

DOROTHY   You don't have a job, remember?

ROSE   I haven't forgotton, Dorothy. I've just been too
          busy to start looking.

DOROTHY   You haven't even started looking?

ROSE   Don't worry will you. There's always a job for
          people who aren't afraid of hard work. That's
          what my father used to say.

DOROTHY   He was talking about milking cows in Minne-
          sota.

(Sophia enters with phone messages)

SOPHIA   *(To Rose)* Here. Phone messages.

ROSE   Oh, thank you.

SOPHIA   If you have to go out tomorrow, ask those crybabies not to call during "The Young and the Restless".

ROSE   *(Reads messages)* Mr. Wyner's depressed ... Mrs. Gibson's despondent ...Mrs. Duvalier's been deported. Why, oh why, can't grief take a holiday?

DOROTHY   Oh, it does, Rose. It does. Eventually it comes to Miami like everyone else. My god, I don't believe it. Barry Glick is in town. Oh, I haven't seen him since high school. Barry Glick. Ma, Ma, Ma, look, Barry Glick. Oh, boy, did I have the hots for him. He says he wants to get together next week.

SOPHIA   Are you going to see him?

DOROTHY   See him? If he's within fifty pounds of where he used to be, I'm going to marry him. Oh, Barry Glick.

ROSE   Oh, Mrs. Montes found her cat. I'll bet she's happy, too.

SOPHIA   Not exactly. She found it under a Jeep Wagoneer.

ACT ONE
Scene 3

NIGHT. ONE WEEK LATER
HALLWAY

(After Midnight. The hallway is dark and empty. Dorothy exits her bedroom. She crosses hallway to Rose's bedroom door and knocks)

DOROTHY	Rose? . . . Rose? *(There is no response)* ROSE'S BEDROOM – CONTINUOUS ACTION *(Rose is sound asleep. Dorothy enters and switches on light)* Rose, will you wake up. You have a call.
ROSE	Is it time to milk the cows, Daddy?
DOROTHY	No, kitten, you have a phone call. *(Rose removes earplugs)*
ROSE	What did you say, Dorothy?
DOROTHY	You have a phone call. It's your friend Milton.
ROSE	Oh. Milton. I can't believe he's calling at this hour.
DOROTHY	You told him to call day or night.
ROSE	I didn't mean it. It's an expression. Like, 'Laugh and the world laughs with you'. Well, the whole world doesn't really laugh.
DOROTHY	That's because they're too busy calling here in the middle of the night. Goodnight, Rose. HALLWAY – CONTINUOUS ACTION *(Dorothy enters from Rose's bedroom. Blanche is standing in her doorway)*
BLANCHE	I hate phone calls in the middle of the night. Now I'll never get back to sleep. *(She starts down hallway)* I'm as jumpy as a virgin at a prison rodeo.
DOROTHY	Boy, that's pretty jumpy. *(Following Blanche)* LIVING ROOM – CONTINUOUS ACTION
BLANCHE	Well, didn't the phone scare you?
DOROTHY	*(Switching on light)* Well, of course it did. It's one of those times I miss having a man around. They're so good at answering the phone in the

middle of the night.

BLANCHE   *(Smiles)* That's not all they're good at.
(Sophia has been sitting unnoticed in an armchair off to the side)

SOPHIA   And when they're really good, you don't even hear the phone.

DOROTHY   Ma! Ma. Why are you sitting here in the dark? *(She switches on lamp)*

SOPHIA   Why not? I've seen the living room before.

DOROTHY   I have to get some rest. Tomorrow I am seeing Barry Phil Glick for the first time in thirty-five years. If I don't get at least six hours sleep I look like Buddy Ebsen.

BLANCHE   Now that you mention it . . .

DOROTHY   Shut up, Blanche.

BLANCHE   Oh, I know it. You're right. It's just terrible. If I get up in the middle of the night, I eat.

DOROTHY   Wait a minute. You know something, we're being selfish. I mean, Rose's problem is more important than my date.

BLANCHE   Or my losing two pounds.

SOPHIA   Three pounds.

DOROTHY   She has to face reality.

BLANCHE   I am. I already lost one pound.

SOPHIA   In your dreams.

DOROTHY   I'm talking about Rose. She has to find a job. She's been out of work for over a week.
(Rose enters)

ROSE   I am really sorry about this, girls. It won't happen again. Now c'mon. We can all go back to sleep now.

(She starts to exit)

DOROTHY   No, no, no. Wait. Rose, sit down. Move over. Move over. Now listen. We have something to talk to you about. We are worried about you. Now maybe it's none of our business, but all that time that you spend with those pathetic wimps from the Centre, you should spend looking for a job.

ROSE   But those wimps need me.

BLANCHE   But Rose, honey, you have your own problems.

DOROTHY   Look, you're fifty-five, unemployed, your husband is dead and you have no training.

BLANCHE   Let's face it, Rose, you're not exactly Mary Lou Retton. Honey, we know it's not easy, but you've got to get out there and try.

ROSE   I have tried. I just haven't told you. I've had dozens of job interviews since the Centre closed. No one wants me. I need something to do with my life. I never think of myself as old but everyone else does. Maybe I am old. Old and useless . . .and terrified.
(Rose quickly exits room. Dorothy and Blanche exchange looks)

END OF ACT ONE

ACT TWO
Scene 1

ROSE'S
BEDROOM – MOMENTS LATER

ROSE'S BEDROOM
(Rose is lying on her bed)

KNOCK AT DOOR

ROSE   Come in.
(Dorothy and Blanche enter)

DOROTHY   Oh, Rose. Rose, honey, now why didn't you tell us what was going on?

ROSE   Because you can't help me find a job. Because nobody or nothing can make me young again.

DOROTHY   Oh, all right, Rose, so your life isn't the same as it used to be. The rules have changed. But it's happened before, hasn't it? I mean, what did you do after Charlie died?

ROSE   Buried him.

DOROTHY   I mean, what did you do the next day? When you had to start putting your life together.

ROSE   I couldn't do it. I'd been a housewife for thirty-two years. I totally depended on Charlie.

DOROTHY   Yeah, but the point is, eventually you did what you had to do. You took care of yourself. Sweetheart, you're now in exactly the same position.

ROSE   Not 'exactly'. I'm five years older. And nobody wants me around.

BLANCHE   Oh, honey, we want you around. We just can't afford to pay you.

DOROTHY   Look, Rose, Rose, look at me. Rose, listen. You are feeling sorry for yourself. Sure, you're five years older. So am I. So is Blanche. Alright, so you have a few more wrinkles. So do I. So has Blanche. Alright, you're a little thicker around the middle. So is Blanche. Listen, we are not about to stand by and just let you give up. We're going to figure out what it is you're doing wrong on your interviews. Then we're gonna fix it, and we're gonna try to get you some more appointments.

ROSE	Appointments are the easy part. I've got one tomorrow. I'd kill for this job. Hospital Administrator. But I'll never get it. I'm not qualified. I'm too old.
DOROTHY	What time is your appointment?
ROSE	Eight-thirty.
DOROTHY	Let me see your resumé. *(Rose takes resumé from attaché case and hands it to Dorothy)* C'mon, c'mon, c'mon. Okay, now let's see. Let's see . . . Home Ec major at Rockport Community College . . . Six months at St. Paul's Business School . . . Thirty-two years of marriage . . . Laid off from your job at grief counselling. Hobbies: cheese making, stamp collecting and Viking History. Rose, this stinks.
ROSE	But it's the truth.
DOROTHY	Honey, sometimes you have to stretch the truth. Wait a minute. Of course you do. Now let's see. *(Correcting with pencil)* Graduated top of your class . . . Intensive Post-graduate Study. Thirty-two years with the same employer until you moved to Miami. Currently seeking work in the private sector. Voila! This is the resumé of a potential Hospital Administrator.
ROSE	Well, I don't know if I can pull it off, but I'm willing to give it a try.
DOROTHY	Oh, good. Now we can get some sleep.
BLANCHE	Oh, I can't fall asleep now.
DOROTHY	What? Still at the Rodeo, Blanche?

ROSE	I can't sleep either. Why don't I make us all some warm milk. *(Rose, Blanche and Dorothy exit)* *LIVING ROOM – CONTINUOUS ACTION* *(Rose, Dorothy and Blanche enter)*
ROSE	After I drink it, I go right to sleep.
BLANCHE	I can think of something else after which I go right to sleep, huh, Dorothy?
DOROTHY	During. *(They go into kitchen)*
ROSE	Girls, we can't drink plain milk.
BLANCHE	Why not?
ROSE	It's disgusting. If we're gonna have milk, we need cookies. *(They all stand there dead still, exchange looks for a few beats, then make a beeline for the cookies)*
BLANCHE	Hell, if I'm gonna have cookies, I'm gonna have cheesecake.
ROSE	If there's cheesecake?
BLANCHE	Chocolate cheesecake.
DOROTHY	You bought chocolate cheesecake?
BLANCHE	For an emergency.
DOROTHY	What kind of emergency, nuclear war?
BLANCHE	Depression.
ROSE	*(Who's been foraging in the freezer)* Oh, you'll never guess what I found!
DOROTHY	Jimmy Hoffa.
ROSE	Pepperoni.
BLANCHE	Uh-oh.
DOROTHY	Don't tell Mom.

ROSE   That could be an appetizer.
(They have all the food on the table)

BLANCHE   This is good. This is all food that would have spoiled.
(They start eating and eat throughout)

DOROTHY   I am so glad that my date with Barry is tomorrow. The fat won't have time to show.

ROSE   It won't?

DOROTHY   No. It always takes a few days before it shows.

ROSE   Where does it go in the meantime?

DOROTHY   To Connecticut. How do I know where it goes?

BLANCHE   With me, the minute it goes in my mouth, I balloon up. I can go out to dinner and in the middle of the meal my pants are cutting off my circulation so bad my feet are turning blue.

DOROTHY   I just want to be svelte for Barry.

ROSE   Barry Glick is very important to you.

DOROTHY   Ahh, Barry was the man I wanted to be the first.

ROSE   First where?

DOROTHY   On Mars, Rose. My first lover.

BLANCHE   Well, so, what happened?

DOROTHY   Stanley. That's what happened. Stanley. I went to a drive-in with Stanley. He said he was being shipped off to Korea and would probably die and it would mean so much. That was my part of the war effort. It took three seconds. I wasn't sure that we had done anything actually until nine months later when the baby came, then I figured out that we had. You know, that was my only proof.

ROSE	I waited till my wedding night.
BLANCHE	No.
ROSE	Yes.
DOROTHY	And?
ROSE	And . . . It was a surprise.
BLANCHE	How is that possible? Another man showed up?
ROSE	What I mean is, I had never *seen* a man before.
BLANCHE	A *man*?
ROSE	You know . . . a man.
BLANCHE	No.
ROSE	Yes.
DOROTHY	What about your father? You mean you never saw your father?
ROSE	My father? Oh, no! My father! Oh, my goodness, no. Oh, I would have simply, well . . . oh . . . my . . .
BLANCHE/ DOROTHY	Easy, easy, easy, Rose. Calm down, calm down. Alright.
ROSE	The only things I ever saw were the animals on the farm. You know, the bulls, the horses . . .
BLANCHE	Tough act to follow.
ROSE	Actually, that first night I was kind of . . . well . . . appalled, I guess. But Charlie was very patient. It was really very nice once I understood that that's really what you were supposed to do and it wasn't some colossal joke, you know? *(Dorothy coughs)* I mean, didn't you think it was a ridiculous thing to do at first?
BLANCHE	No. Well, I certainly didn't wait for my

wedding night, honey. I couldn't. I had these urges. You know, in the South we mature faster. I think it's the heat.

DOROTHY   I think it's the gin.

BLANCHE   Anyhow, my first was Billy. Oh, I remember it so well, just like it was yesterday. That night under the dogwood trees, the air thick with perfume and me with Billy . . .Or Bobby. Yeah, Bobby. It was Bobby . . .or was it Ben? Oh, who knows. Anyway, it started with a B.

ROSE   That first time, did you have . . .

BLANCHE   Are you serious? Why many times that time. Many, many times.

ROSE   You did?

BLANCHE   You didn't?

ROSE   No. Oh, it was nice. Being near Charlie was always nice, but it was five years before I knew what made your eyes go back in your head. Dorothy, did you have . . .uh . . .?

DOROTHY   How could I? I mean it always seemed to happen before I was in the room.

ROSE   Look what we've eaten.

BLANCHE   Oh, and I can't sleep on a full stomach.

DOROTHY   Would you look at what time it is. Would you like some coffee?

ROSE   Sure. How about danish? It's almost breakfast.

BLANCHE   Hey, want some eggs?

DOROTHY   Do we have bacon?

ROSE   Yeah.

DOROTHY   Scramble me a couple.

BLANCHE   Scramble some.

ACT TWO
Scene 2

LANAI – LATE AFTERNOON
(Blanche and Milton sit whispering and laughing)

MILTON   You're a wonderful woman, Blanche. No offense to Rose, but I'm glad she wasn't here when I dropped by today.

BLANCHE   Why, Milton, what a sweet thing to say. That must be why I date more than she does.

MILTON   And I meant what I said about that diet of yours. Men of our generation like a little meat on their woman. Maybe . . .uh . . . you don't want to pinch an inch, but I do.
(He gives her a pinch, then starts to exit)

BLANCHE   Oh, Milton.

MILTON   See you tonight at seven.
(Sophia enters from the living room as Milton crosses in opposite direction)

BLANCHE   Tonight at seven, Milton.

MILTON   *(To Sophia, as he exits)* Good afternoon.

SOPHIA   I thought he belonged to the other one.

BLANCHE   Well, I'm sure Rose won't mind one bit.

SOPHIA   He's a man. It's not like sharing a yogurt.
(Dorothy enters)

DOROTHY   Hello, hello, hello. Hi, Ma.

BLANCHE   Hi, Dorothy.

DOROTHY   Honey, did Barry call?

BLANCHE   Not that I know of.

DOROTHY   Oh, we're supposed to go out again.

BLANCHE   Oh, It sounds like lunch went well.

DOROTHY   Oh, we had such fun. You know, Barry is exactly as I remembered him.

BLANCHE   Oh, come on now. After thirty-five years there must have been some surprises.

DOROTHY   Well, a few. You know, his hair's a little thinner . . . he's put on a little weight . . .

BLANCHE   But is he still your fantasy lover or has fantasy become a reality?

DOROTHY   Well, not exactly. You see, Barry Glick . . . is gay.

SOPHIA   I knew he was gay. I could tell by the way he used to worship Buster Crabbe.
         (*Sophia exits*)

BLANCHE   (*To Dorothy*) Oh, honey, are you just devastated?

DOROTHY   Oh, hey, what the hell. I mean, if I can't have him, at least I know no other woman can have him either.
         (*Rose enters, cheerfully*)

ROSE   Hi, girls.
       (*Ad-lib hellos*)

DOROTHY   Are we to assume from your cheerful demeanour that we are talking to a new Hospital Administrator?

ROSE   (*Still cheerful*) Not even close.

BLANCHE   Well what'd you do? Take an anti-depressant?

ROSE   Oh, don't be silly. But I was depressed. Incredibly depressed. I didn't know which way to turn or where to go. So I stopped in at the coffee shop at the Fountain Rock for a root-beer float to make me feel better. They make a terrific root-beer float. They have that old fashioned root-beer syrup . . .

DOROTHY	Look, Rose, get off the float. Get to the point.
ROSE	Well, after I drank it, I started to get sad again and then I saw the answer right in front of me.
DOROTHY	What? What? What?
ROSE	A 'help wanted' sign.
DOROTHY	And? And?
ROSE	I am a waitress at the Fountain Rock Coffee Shop. It's twelve hours a day, four days a week, minimum wage and tips and a sixty percent employee discount on day-old danish.
BLANCHE	A coffee shop?
DOROTHY	Day-old danish?
BLANCHE	Twelve hour days in a steamy, hash joint serving chili to a bunch of grubby truckers.
DOROTHY	Oh, come on, Blanche, she's working at the Fountain Rock. It's not Mel's Diner. I mean, the worst that can happen is she'll get scratched by a pinky ring.
BLANCHE	But twelve hours on your feet waiting tables. Honey, that is gritty, grimy gruelling work.
ROSE	But it's work. It beats the hell out of feeling sorry for myself. And it'll be a whole lot nicer to fall asleep from being tired than crying.
DOROTHY	Of course it will. Oh, Rose honey. Rose, I am so happy for you.
BLANCHE	Well, heck. If you're happy, then I'm happy, too.
ROSE	Oh, thank you for seeing me through this.
BLANCHE	Honey, I want to ask you about Milton. From the Centre?
ROSE	Yes?

BLANCHE   Well, now that is strictly a professional relationship . . . ?

ROSE   Oh, absolutely. Oh, there couldn't be anything between me and Milton. He has this thing about only dating fat women.
(Rose and Dorothy exit, chatting, as Blanche reacts)

END OF ACT TWO

TRANSPLANT

Written by: SUSAN HARRIS
Directed by: PAUL BOGART

· *Introduction* ·

T HE EVER-FLIRTING BLANCHE (Rue McClanahan), whose thrusting chest and pert wiggle are amusingly at odds with her 50-plus years, is often merely a reminder that middle-aged lust is not just a possibility but a healthy alternative to a dozy life of TV dinners.

Yet in *Transplant*, writer Susan Harris, who also created the series, makes Blanche the primary focus of aggressive sibling rivalry and the need to solve it before death.

The build-up to her sister Virginia's arrival is typically amusing; a device used to lull us into comfort before yanking the rug out from under our feet. After much preamble about the hate-hate relationship between Blanche and Virginia, Sophia walks on to crack a few acid one-liners:

Rose: "Sophia, if you hated your sister, would you clean the house?"

Sophia: "I'd put vaseline on the tips of her walker."

Blanche, for once putting frivolity and sex on the back burner, is frozen by paranoia at the thought of Virginia arriving. So, breathing spite, she announces to Rose:

"She was the adorable one, the gorgeous one, the brilliant one. She sat in my Daddy's lap for sixteen years. Oh, and she was hateful. You know what she would do? She used to bite herself on the arm and then run crying to Daddy that I had done it. And he'd punish me. Oh, she got me in trouble all the time. Daddy used to call me the bad seed."

After much withering sarcasm about her sister's weight,

ageing skin and marriage to a boyfriend of Blanche's, Blanche has her expectations upended by Virginia's decency and warmth and by her blunt confession that she will die unless she finds a kidney donor.

The two serious issues of sisterly friction and organ transplants are bolted together in a frank, uninhibited and unsentimental way. Free of the syrup and schmaltz of most TV sitcoms, Virginia's problem is introduced in an almost offhand manner.

Dorothy: "I mean the woman is dying. What could she possibly want from you?"

Blanche: "My kidney."

However, to draw the viewer towards these tough issues, even the most harrowing dialogue is laced with surreal put-downs about vasectomies, feeding kidneys to cats and donating them to dogs. Making a fetching contrast with matters of old age and death is the sub-text about a friend's baby whom the ladies have to mind for a while. As the possibility of Virginia's demise is discussed, the reality of ageing woman trying to recall how to treat babies is woven into the text to lighten the load. As ever, comedy and poignancy make suitable bedfellows.

CAST
Dorothy, Rose, Blanche, Sophia, Virginia, Waiter.

ACT ONE
Scene 1

Living Room – Day

(*Rose and Blanche are cleaning*)

BLANCHE	Oh, it's a mess. This place is just a mess. Rose, what am I going to do? She's gonna be here any minute. This place is a pig sty.
ROSE	(*Rises*) Blanche, it looks gorgeous. (*About to sit on couch*)
BLANCHE	Don't sit. I just fluffed. Dust the table.
ROSE	I just did.
BLANCHE	Well, do it again. God, I wish she wasn't coming. I just hate her.
ROSE	I can't believe you hate your sister.
BLANCHE	I despise her. Oh, I wish I'd gotten a decorator. Nancy Reagan's decorator. That would kill my sister.
ROSE	(*Dusts chair*) She's your sister. How can you hate your sister?
BLANCHE	Because she made me and my big sister Charmain miserable our entire lives.
ROSE	I never heard of such a thing.
BLANCHE	You never heard of anybody hating their sister?
ROSE	Never. Maybe it's Southern.
BLANCHE	Sleeping with your brothers is Southern. Dust, Rose, dust. We're running out of time.

(Sophia enters)

ROSE   Sophia, if you hated your sister, would you clean the house?

SOPHIA   I'd put vaseline on the tips of her walker. *(Dorothy enters with baby)*

DOROTHY   Everybody, look what I have.

ROSE   Where did you find . . .

BLANCHE   Don't sit. Don't sit.

ROSE   *(To baby)* Oh, what is our name?

DOROTHY   Danny.

BLANCHE   Dorothy, what in the world is that?

DOROTHY   It's a flounder, Blanche. What do you think it is?

BLANCHE   What's the baby doing here?

DOROTHY   It's Lucy and Ted's baby. Ted had a little accident water skiing. Lucy's taking him to the hospital.

BLANCHE   Now we cannot have a baby in this house. My sister's coming.

DOROTHY   Does she eat them?

BLANCHE   Dorothy, I have cleaned this house from top to bottom. I have killed myself for two days. Now, babies make a mess.

DOROTHY   In diapers. And unless we use them as placemats, your sister'll never know.

BLANCHE   Oh, Lord.

ROSE   *(To baby)* Utchy butchy butchy boo. Utchy butchy butchy boo. Butchy boo. Butchy boo.

SOPHIA   Finally someone she can talk to.

BLANCHE   I just hope it doesn't make a fuss when my sister's here.

DOROTHY	I thought you hate this sister who's coming.
BLANCHE	I do.
DOROTHY	I'm going to put him to bed. Ma, the babas.

(Dorothy exits, Sophia follows)

ROSE	Why do you hate your sister that's what I'd want to know.
BLANCHE	Because when she was born, I ceased to exist. I never saw my Mama and Daddy again.
ROSE	Where did they go?
BLANCHE	They never looked at me again, Rose. She was the adorable one, the gorgeous one, the brilliant one. She sat in my Daddy's lap for sixteen years. Oh, and she was hateful. You know what she would do? She used to bite herself on the arm and then run crying to Daddy that I had done it. And he'd punish me. Oh, she got me in trouble all the time. Daddy used to call me the bad seed.

(Sophia exits)

Once she even electrocuted me.

ROSE	Oh, no.
BLANCHE	Oh, yes. It was the day before Christmas and we were playing. And she jiggled the tree and the star fell off and broke. So, she told me to pick it up and put it on my finger. And I did. Then she plugged it in and wham! My eyes bugged out; my hair shot straight up, I did a crazy rubber dance all over the room. I'm sure my heart even stopped beating for a minute. Then she ran to Daddy and told him that I had broken the star and almost electrocuted *her*. And he sent me to my room for all of Christmas Eve and told me that the Baby Jesus was mad at me for ruining His birthday.

ROSE   Oh, Blanche, that's horrible.

BLANCHE And that's not the worst part. That darn electricity straightened my hair. I used to have curly hair.
(She cleans wall)

ACT ONE
Scene 2

LIVING ROOM – LATER THAT DAY
(Blanche and Virginia enter)

VIRGINIA That was a lovely lunch, Blanche. A lovely lunch, in a lovely house with your lovely friends.

BLANCHE Stop making fun of me, Virginia.

VIRGINIA Making fun of you . . .Honey, I was complimenting you.

BLANCHE I heard the way you said "lovely".

VIRGINIA How did I say "lovely"?
(They sit)

BLANCHE Oh, you know very well how you said "lovely". You said "lovely" the same way you say "lovely" to a date who's just shown up in a light blue tuxedo.

VIRGINIA Well, I meant lovely. No matter how it came out.

BLANCHE I guess maybe I just didn't think you'd recognize good taste. You know this house was done by Nancy Reagan's decorator.

VIRGINIA Really?

BLANCHE Yes. But never mind about that. Let's talk about you. You look like you've lost weight, sugah.

VIRGINIA	I have.
BLANCHE	You know, at your age when you lose weight your skin just hangs there like leaves on a willow.
VIRGINIA	I haven't lost that much. I don't think that's happened yet.
BLANCHE	Well, I don't know, but if I were you I sure wouldn't wave goodbye. *(Indicates underarm flab)*
VIRGINIA	And if I were you I sure wouldn't jog without a mumu. *(Does a bouncing gesture)*
BLANCHE	Is that so? Well, just let me tell you something . . .
VIRGINIA	Oh, please. Let's not do this. Let's grow up, for God's sake. We have done this our whole lives long. Let's call an end to it. Okay?
BLANCHE	Sure, whatever. *(A beat)* So. You're thinking of getting a face lift . . . for your, uh . . . how do I put this delicately . . . *(She flaps under the chin)* . . . turkey wattle or what?

<u>ACT ONE</u>
<u>Scene 3</u>

DOROTHY'S BEDROOM – *LATER*
(Rose and Sophia are there. Dorothy holds the baby)

BABY CRY	
DOROTHY	There, there.
ROSE	It's colic. My children had it. You give them brandy.

SOPHIA   For colic?

DOROTHY   Yes. After dinner. With a cigar. Rose, you give brandy for teething; you rub it on their gums.

ROSE   Oh. I thought I gave it to them for colic. In their bottles. But my babies were very happy.

SOPHIA   Put it in my bottle; I'll be happy, too.

ROSE   Look at this. Pop-ups. Isn't that wonderful? Remember, when we had to use cotton and fish ointment?
(She makes a face)

SOPHIA   That's nothing. In Sicily, we used a leaf and the river.

DOROTHY   Ma, you never had a baby in Sicily.

SOPHIA   I *was* a baby in Sicily.

ROSE   Disposable bottles and formula. We had to sterilize our bottles and make the formula.

SOPHIA   I nursed. Your brother was twelve when he stopped. He wanted to come home from school at lunchtime. I got nothing left up here.

DOROTHY   Oh, Ma.
(Blanche appears in doorway and enters)

BLANCHE   Well, she's gone.

DOROTHY   That's it? That's why we couldn't sit on a couch for two days?

BLANCHE   No. I have to have dinner with her tonight. Why is that baby still here?

DOROTHY   *(Sits)* Oh, well, they're still at the hospital. It's taking a little longer than they thought.

ROSE   Blanche, your sister seemed very nice.

BLANCHE   She was nicer than she's ever been. She was interested, charming, caring, loving. Just couldn't have been more wonderful. I just wonder what she wants, the conniving little witch.

ACT ONE
Scene 4

Restaurant – That Night
(Blanche and Virginia are there)

BLANCHE   *(To waiter)* You're welcome, Maurice.

VIRGINIA   Let's make a toast.

BLANCHE   With water?

VIRGINIA   Well, I can't drink.

BLANCHE   You never could. One Jack Daniels, and you disappear with half a fraternity house.

VIRGINIA   Blanche, we said we weren't going to do this.

BLANCHE   Well, what else can we do; we never had a real conversation our entire lives.

VIRGINIA   Well then, it's time for us to start. Okay?

BLANCHE   Fine with me.

VIRGINIA   *(Toasts)* To us. To the beginning of a new and wonderful relationship. To sisters.

BLANCHE   That's very sweet, Virginia. Now what do you *want*?

VIRGINIA   What is it with you? You just step on any kind of tender moment.

BLANCHE   Tender moment, my foot. All my life you've taken everything that ever meant anything to me.

VIRGINIA   What did I take? A couple of cashmere sweaters and a poodle skirt?

BLANCHE	*(A beat)* You took my poodle skirt? Was that you?
VIRGINIA	Blanche, that was over forty years ago.
BLANCHE	Oh, shut up.
VIRGINIA	I can't believe that you are still crazy over that.
BLANCHE	It's not over that. It's over Tom.
VIRGINIA	Tom?
BLANCHE	Don't act so surprised, Virginia. You knew I was dating him. Then I had to go to the country to visit Aunt Augusta. When I got back I had poison ivy and you had Tom. I loved that boy. I wanted to marry him. We were serious.
VIRGINIA	But you'd only had two dates with him.
BLANCHE	I was fast.
VIRGINIA	I swear I didn't think that you liked him at all.
BLANCHE	Then I had to be Maid of Honour at your wedding and I had to stand there and watch you marry Tom *and* I had to wear that green dress which you knew was my most awful colour. I looked like a swamp frog. Everyone I ever loved, you took.
VIRGINIA	Would it help you to know that Tom fooled around?
BLANCHE	No. *(A beat)* With who?
VIRGINIA	Everyone.
BLANCHE	Huh . . . Serves you right.
VIRGINIA	Blanche . . .
BLANCHE	Well, it does. What goes around, comes around.

VIRGINIA	Well, then I must have been *really* bad.
BLANCHE	What do you mean?
VIRGINIA	Well, it's the reason I'm here.
BLANCHE	I knew it. I knew you had a reason. It better be a good one.
VIRGINIA	I'm dying.
BLANCHE	What?
VIRGINIA	I'm dying.
BLANCHE	Well. My God. (*Long beat*) That explains it then.
VIRGINIA	What?
BLANCHE	Why you're looking so much older than I am.

ACT ONE
Scene 5

LIVING ROOM – LATER THAT NIGHT
(*Dorothy and Sophia are there. Dorothy is reading, Sophia eats Fritos*)

DOROTHY	Ma, could you eat a little more quietly, please?
SOPHIA	These are Fritos. You want me to swallow them whole? (*Blanche enters*)
BLANCHE	Hi everybody.
DOROTHY	Hi Blanche.
BLANCHE	(*Crosses up centre*) Oh, is the baby gone?
DOROTHY	No. Rose is out driving him around to get him to sleep.

BLANCHE	Why is he still here?
DOROTHY	Well, Ted needs minor surgery so they're still at the hospital. Oh, what about Virginia?
BLANCHE	Well? *(Rose enters with baby in car seat)*
ROSE	Sshhhh.
DOROTHY	Is he asleep? *(Rose nods)* Do you need help?
ROSE	No.
BLANCHE	We're gonna have this baby 'til college.
ROSE	Sshhh. *(Rose exits with baby)*
DOROTHY	*(To Blanche)* So, how was dinner?
BLANCHE	I'm still in shock.
DOROTHY	What happened?
BLANCHE	I just can't believe it.
DOROTHY	What?
BLANCHE	You know you just never think you're gonna hear that.
DOROTHY	Blanche. Tell me.
BLANCHE	She's dying.
DOROTHY	What?
BLANCHE	My sister's dying. *(Rose enters)*
ROSE	What?
SOPHIA	Dying. She's dying.
ROSE	*(Kneels)* Oh my God, Blanche, honey. I didn't even know you were sick.
DOROTHY	Not Blanche. Her sister.

ROSE	Oh, thank God.
DOROTHY	And she came to tell you, is that it?
BLANCHE	No, please. She could have done that with a phone call. No, it was just like I said. She wanted something.
DOROTHY	Oh, please, enough already. I mean the woman is dying. What could she possibly want from you?
BLANCHE	My kidney.

END OF ACT ONE

ACT TWO
Scene 1

LIVING ROOM – CONTINUOUS ACTION

DOROTHY	Your kidney?
BLANCHE	My kidney.
ROSE	Why would she need a kidney?
DOROTHY	To feed the cat, Rose.
BLANCHE	She's going into renal failure. So a transplant is her best hope.
DOROTHY	Oh, honey, I'm so sorry.
ROSE	What happens if she doesn't get your kidney?
BLANCHE	She'll die.
ROSE	You hold her life in your hands. What are you gonna do?
BLANCHE	I don't know.
SOPHIA	I'm glad you're not my sister. (*They all look at Sophia*)
BLANCHE	I need something to eat.

(They all go into the kitchen)

ROSE   Well, didn't you just have dinner?

BLANCHE   Oh, I couldn't eat. I was just too stunned.

DOROTHY   What are you going to do, Blanche?

BLANCHE   Oh, I don't know. I mean it isn't as if she were my daughter. She's my sister. My sister that I *hate*.

SOPHIA   I wish I could give her my kidneys. Let *her* get up all night.

BLANCHE   And what if I gave her my kidney and then the one good kidney I have left stops working? What do I do then, ask for my kidney back?

ROSE   You'd be an Indian Giver.

BLANCHE   I need both my kidneys. You know what'll happen if I give her one? My ankles will swell, my eyes will puff up. I'll look just like The Pillsbury Dough Boy.

DOROTHY   Blanche, that does not happen. You can live just fine with one kidney.

BLANCHE   I can't eat this food. I'm going to bed. I'll just think about it tomorrow.
(Goes to door)
All I know is girls, I'm in a no win situation here. I lose a sister or a kidney. Either way, no matter what I do, I'm gonna lose something.
(Blanche exits)

ROSE   What would you do?

DOROTHY   Well, for my children I wouldn't even have to think. I mean, I'd give 'em both my kidneys. I'd cut them out myself.

ROSE   Me, too: I'd give them my heart.

SOPHIA   I'd give to all my children. Except Phil.

DOROTHY Why not Phil?

SOPHIA Because he never calls, he never writes. I only hear from him at Christmas when he sends me a cheddar cheese nativity scene. I'm Catholic. I can't spread a Wise Man on a Ritz cracker.

ROSE If I still had my dog Fluffy I'd give to him.

SOPHIA You'd give what to Fluffy?

ROSE My kidney.

DOROTHY Oh, come on, Rose. You'd give a kidney to a dog?

ROSE Absolutely.

SOPHIA So he could wizz on your rug?

ROSE I would give to him because of everything he gave to me. He was loving, he was loyal, he was fun, he never left my side.

DOROTHY I wish my ex had been like Fluffy. It would have solved alot of problems.

SOPHIA You could have had him fixed.
(*A beat*)

DOROTHY Oh, poor Blanche.

ACT TWO
Scene 2

LIVING ROOM – NEXT DAY
(*Blanche and Virginia are there*)

VIRGINIA Blanche, I know you need some time to think it over.

BLANCHE (*Pouring coffee*) You're damn right, I do. We're talking about a vital organ of my body here.

VIRGINIA I know.

(Sophia enters)

SOPHIA   *(Crosses to Blanche)* You gonna give it to her or not?

BLANCHE   Sophia . . .

SOPHIA   *(Crosses to kitchen)* What does it mean? A little less bourbon.

VIRGINIA   It's a big decision, Sophia. She's got to think about it.

SOPHIA   She's family. If you can't count on family who the hell can you count on?
(Sophia exits)

BLANCHE   She's Italian.

VIRGINIA   I'll understand . . . you know . . . if you decide not to.

BLANCHE   Well, how come you didn't ask Charmain for her kidney? You were always closer to Charmain.

VIRGINIA   Charmain's kidneys are attached to each other.

BLANCHE   What do you mean, attached?

VIRGINIA   Well, the two are joined. It's like having one big kidney and you can't separate them.

BLANCHE   Leave it to Charmain.

VIRGINIA   I know. She never could help Mama because she had heart flutters and she never could take gym class, no, because she had a tipped uterus. And she never did any housework because she had a spastic colon. Now she has attached kidneys.

BLANCHE   That girl is some kind of mutant.
(Sophia enters again)

SOPHIA   I'd give you one of my kidneys, but I'm sure you'd rather have one you can control.

VIRGINIA	Thank you, Sophia.
SOPHIA	Welcome. (*Sophia exits*)
VIRGINIA	Look, if you decide not to . . . I'll understand. I swear.
BLANCHE	Sure. You'll be dead. And everybody'll say Blanche killed her.
VIRGINIA	What I'm trying to say, is it's a terrible choice I've given you. I don't even know what I would do under the same circumstances.
BLANCHE	Are you saying you mean you don't know if you'd give me your kidney?
VIRGINIA	No. I don't.
BLANCHE	Well, I'm not surprised. You never even lent me a kleenex. Besides, I'm a size eight. Your kidney wouldn't fit me. There's not room in my body for your kidney.
VIRGINIA	Well, I guess I'd better be going. (*They rise*) And if you decide to go ahead with it, I'll see you in Atlanta in a few days.
BLANCHE	Are you scared?
VIRGINIA	Terrified.
BLANCHE	I guess anybody would be.
VIRGINIA	I guess. Blanche, whatever happens – I love you. (*They hug*) Thank you.
BLANCHE	Goodbye. (*Virginia exits*)

ACT TWO
Scene 3

KITCHEN – NEXT DAY

ROSE (*After hanging up phone she crosses to table*) The doctor said it's the first time he's ever been called because a baby was sleeping in the day, and then I think he called me an idiot.

DOROTHY He's sleeping in the day because he has four women who won't let him sleep at night. Now who went in there last night? Was it you? (*Long beat*)

ROSE Well, I went in once.

DOROTHY Why?

ROSE I've been working. I hadn't seen him all day.

DOROTHY And was he sleeping?

ROSE At first.

DOROTHY This has got to stop. No wonder that baby didn't sleep.

BLANCHE He wasn't the only one who was up all night.

ROSE You were, too?

BLANCHE Yes. I had time to do alot of thinking.

DOROTHY And . . .

BLANCHE And, of course I'm going to do it.

DOROTHY Oh, Blanche. You're a brave lady.

ROSE Oh, you really are, honey.

BLANCHE No, I have to. I don't want my sister to die. I want her to live. And not just for her. For me. I want to get to know her like a grown-up. I want us to have a chance to be friends . . . sisters. After all, she's all the family I have.

ROSE   I thought you had a sister Charmain.

BLANCHE   Oh, you can't count her. She's an awful, selfish, neurotic woman who made me and Virginia miserable our entire lives.
(Rises)
I gotta go pack.
(She exits)

ACT TWO
Scene 4

LIVING ROOM – NEXT DAY
(Rose, Sophia, and Dorothy are there. Dorothy holds baby)

DOROTHY   I hate to give him back.

ROSE   Goodbye, Danny. Goodbye, pussycat. Goodbye, little fella. Bye-bye. Bye-bye. Bye-bye.

SOPHIA   What are you carrying on? It's like talking to a salami.

DOROTHY   Well, he has to leave. I'll be right back. Say Byesie-bye.

ROSE   Bye darlin'.
(Dorothy exits)

ROSE   I'm worried about Blanche. I wish she'd let one of us go with her.

SOPHIA   Not me. I hate hospitals. My friend Manny Fishbein went into the hospital a healthy guy. Then, boom-boom, dead. Just like that. In his sleep. Ninety-eight years old. No apparent cause.

ROSE   I don't like hospitals either. They're full of germs. I always hold my breath in the elevators

because there are sick people in the elevators and it's such a small space and once I had to go to the eighth floor of a hospital and the elevator stopped on every floor and I had to hold my breath all that time and I finally fainted and I hit my head and then I had to stay there because I had a concussion and I had to hold my breath all the way down in the elevator to the emergency room then I had to hold my breath in X-ray where they ask you to hold your breath anyway and . . .
(Dorothy enters)

DOROTHY   I have great news.

SOPHIA   Rose, you'll excuse me. We'll get back to your fascinating hospital story later.

DOROTHY   Ted and Lucy said that we could have the baby again next month when they go away for a weekend.

ROSE   Oh, that's wonderful. Oh, I'm so excited.
(Front door opens. It's Blanche)

BLANCHE   Hi, everybody.

DOROTHY   Blanche! What are you doing here? Is something wrong? I mean, we didn't expect you back so soon.

BLANCHE   The best possible thing has happened. I still have both my kidneys and my sister is fine.

DOROTHY   Blanche, how is that possible?

BLANCHE   They couldn't use my kidney. My blood vessels are too small. Well of course they're too small. I've always been very petite.

DOROTHY   Blanche. Virginia?

BLANCHE   Oh, well, the most wonderful thing happened. They found a donor, an excellent match. She was a retired Mormon school teacher.

ROSE   Virginia's so lucky.

BLANCHE   Oh, I'll say. That kidney was showroom new. Why the wildest thing that ever passed through there was Ovaltine.
(*Then*)
But the best part of it was that hunk of a doctor who examined me he's gonna be in Florida in a few weeks.

ROSE   Wherever she goes she finds a man.

SOPHIA   So do hookers.

DOROTHY   Ma.

BLANCHE   But, the most wonderful thing about all of this is Virginia and me. All that time we wasted hating each other from when we were kids. Now we're getting to know each other and, oh, I just love her. I finally have a sister to love. Isn't it funny? Sometimes you have to almost lose somebody before you realize how much they really mean to you. Let's go out and celebrate life. Let's go out and do something crazy.

SOPHIA   Let's fly to Freeport and gamble all night.

DOROTHY   Ma, we can't afford it.

ROSE   Let's drive to Disney World and ride the teacups.

DOROTHY   Too wild, Rose.

BLANCHE   Hey, I know a bar in Cocoa Beach where you can pick up over-the-hill astronauts.
(*The three stare at her*)

ROSE   Or . . . there's some Rocky Road in the freezer.

BLANCHE   Hey, great.

DOROTHY   Now you're talking.
        END OF ACT TWO

BLANCHE AND THE YOUNGER MAN

Written by: STAN ZIMMERMAN &
JAMES BERG
Directed by: JIM DRAKE

· *Introduction* ·

CONCERNS ABOUT ACCEPTANCE and self-acceptance thread their way through this episode from first page to last. While Rose's mother Alma is perfectly at ease with herself as a wise-cracking card-player who once had a three-year fling with an ex-con, Rose herself, who unwittingly reveals how little she knows of her own mother, persists in smothering her like a favourite cat. Blanche, meanwhile, out on a date with a young man called Dirk, has a tough time accepting her steady advance towards deep wrinkles and creaking limbs.

Both situations, less fraught than some which confront the Golden Girls, are delivered with much comic clout. The discussion about Alma's imminent arrival is hilarious:

Sophia: "Then how come Rose ordered her a wheelchair at the airport, a special meal on the plane, and put an oxygen tank in the garage?"

Dorothy: "Maybe she's a disabled welder on a special diet."

When Alma finally arrives, Rose implies that she is deaf by speaking in block capitals and so startling her chums. At the end of a noisy, forced conversation between them all, Alma offers up the key punchline of this scene when she queries: "Which one is hard of hearing?"

At the centre of the saga is the appealing notion that Rose, who is normally perfection writ large, is also flawed. Able only to treat Alma in the spirit of doting, overprotective daughter, she is forced to think about her behaviour.

She is aided by a volley of quick-fire remarks; from Sophia ("It's too bad Rose won't get off her back"), Dorothy ("She's betting on the horses"), to Alma herself ("Rose, I am not a child. I don't need a nap").

The sharp card-games and feisty talk between Sophia and Alma, not to mention their shopping spree in town, finally force Rose to see her mother as she is.

Blanche too is given a hefty jolt towards reality. Eating out with her aerobics teacher, Dirk, she discovers, not an amusing conversationalist and lusty lover, but a narcissistic neanderthal who cares more for his own body than hers. While Blanche is ready to do business with a duck and double Jack Daniels, Dirk demands a plate of watercress. The conversation flows as follows:

Blanche: "So, Dirk, have you read any good books lately?"

Dirk: "Pumping Iron. I saw the movie too. I don't think it did the book justice."

However, it is Dirk's likening of Blanche to his mother which finally flattens her. While Blanche returns home a wiser, if no less raunchy lady, it is Dorothy who not only puts the whole younger-man scenario into perspective through her own surprising experience, but also binds Blanche's and Rose's escapades together with her customary common sense:

Dorothy: "This is the only peace and quiet I have had in two days. Blanche thinks she's Peter Pan, and Rose has turned into Mommie Dearest."

CAST
DOROTHY, ROSE, BLANCHE, SOPHIA, ALMA, DIRK, WAITER.

ACT ONE
Scene 1

LIVING ROOM – DAY
(Sophia enters from kitchen with food. Sneaks toward hallway. Dorothy enters from hallway)

DOROTHY   Ma, where are you going with all that food?

SOPHIA   I'm taking it to my room.

DOROTHY   Who have you got in there, Shelley Winters?

SOPHIA   I'm stashing it away from Rose's mother. She's on a special diet. I hate those people. You turn your back one second. Your food is gone. Anything on your plate is suddenly on their diet.
KITCHEN – CONTINUOUS

DOROTHY   Ma, please. You haven't even met Rose's mother.

SOPHIA   Believe me. I know a lot of old people. They're all the same. They're cranky. They're demanding. They repeat themselves. They're cranky.

DOROTHY   What makes you think Rose's mother is old? She's the same age as you.

SOPHIA   You're kidding? Then how come Rose ordered her a wheelchair at the airport, a special meal on the plane, and put an oxygen tank in the garage?

DOROTHY   Maybe, she's a disabled welder on a special diet.

(*A beat*)
Ma, be nice to her. Maybe you could even take her out to see some sights.

DOOR CLOSING IN LIVING ROOM

DOROTHY That must be them.

SOPHIA (*Crossing towards living room*) Sure, you three go to work and I get to be the tour guide. This'll be my two-hundredth visit to the Seaquarium. I know the show by heart.

DOROTHY Good. Maybe they'll let you accompany the otters on the xylophone.
(*Sophia exits and Dorothy follows*)
LIVING ROOM – CONTINUOUS
(*Blanche in doorway, with Dirk. Dorothy and Sophia enter*)

BLANCHE Thanks again for the ride home, Dirk. See you at Tuesday's jazzercise class.

DIRK Okay, Blanche. See you then. Unless I see you before then. I mean if you wouldn't mind, maybe we could go out?

BLANCHE Why Dirk, did I just hear you ask me for a date?

SOPHIA What are you, deaf? I heard him from over here.

DIRK So, Blanche, do you think maybe we could have dinner Saturday night?

BLANCHE Why don't I check my date book and let you know?

DIRK Sure, Blanche. I'll call you tomorrow.
(*Dirk exits*)

BLANCHE Well, isn't this an interesting turn of events. I don't know what to do. He *is* a little younger than I am but I hate to break his heart. He's so adorable and he's obviously smitten. But he's

just a boy. He probably doesn't make much
money. But then again . . .

DOROTHY Blanche, the man asked you to have dinner,
not his baby.
(Rose and Alma enter)

ROSE Watch your step, Mother. That's a girl.

ALMA I haven't been a girl since 1912.

ROSE *(Extra loud)* Why, look who's here. I'd like you
all to meet my mother, Mrs. Lindstrom.
Mother, this is Blanche, Dorothy and Sophia.

DOROTHY *(Also loud)* Nice to meet you. How was your
trip!

ALMA *(Yelling)* It was fine!
(To Rose)
Which one is hard of hearing?

ROSE No one is, Mother. We just don't want *you* to
have to strain to hear *us*.

ALMA There's nothing wrong with my ears.

ROSE *(Patronisingly)* Of course there isn't. Why don't
you sit down and I'll bring you a little snack?

BLANCHE *(To Alma)* How long will you be visiting with
us, Mrs. Lindstrom?

ROSE Only a week. Then she's on to Houston to visit
my brother.

SOPHIA *(To Rose)* Is your name Mrs. Lindstrom?

ROSE No . . .

BLANCHE Mrs. Lindstrom, how would you like a little
tour of our home while Rose is fixing your
snack?

ROSE *(Again, before Alma can answer)* I don't think
now's a good time, Blanche. Mother's had a big
day. I don't want her to overdo it.

DOROTHY	She can skip the East Wing, Rose.
ROSE	Maybe tomorrow. Mother, why don't you take a nap while I fix you something to eat?
ALMA	Rose, I'm not a child. I don't need a nap.
ROSE	Mother, there's nothing wrong with taking a nap. Bob Hope takes naps.
DOROTHY	Well, unless he's in the bedroom taking one now, I'm sure she'd rather stay with us.
ROSE	*(Shaking her head)* Dorothy, please. I know what's best for my mother. *(To Alma)* C'mon now, Mother. Let's get you unpacked. *(Rose and Alma exit)*
DOROTHY	She seems like a very nice lady.
SOPHIA	Yeah. It's too bad Rose won't get off her back.
BLANCHE	It's amazing. Amazing. Just amazing.
DOROTHY	What's amazing?
BLANCHE	I am.
DOROTHY	Oh, knock it off.
BLANCHE	I've decided I can handle this relationship. I'm going out with Dirk Saturday night.
DOROTHY	Was it ever in doubt?
BLANCHE	Momentarily. This is strictly off the record, but Dirk is nearly five years younger than I am.
DOROTHY	In what, Blanche? Dog years?
BLANCHE	However, I've decided to overlook that minor detail and succumb to the Vesuvius of passion that is about to erupt from my innermost being.
SOPHIA	Stand back! I think we're going to get something on us.
BLANCHE	I'm talking about what's happening between me

and Dirk. It's something special. Something fragile and rare. I've only felt it once before. It was during my seventeenth summer, when I was working behind the cosmetics counter at the Rexall drugstore. I was stocking the Maybelline display when I heard a booming voice say, "Excuse me, Miss, where are the cuticle scissors?" I turned around and there he was. It's got to be the same feeling the first time you see God. Our eyes locked and for one brief moment there was no one else on earth except the two of us.

DOROTHY Blanche, please. Sidney Sheldon tells shorter stories.

BLANCHE I know in my heart if I had acted on my feelings that day at the Rexall drugstore, today I would be the widow of . . . Mister Chet Huntley . . . I promise you, I'm not going to make the same mistake with Dirk that I made with Chet. (*Blanche exits*)

DOROTHY Didn't she tell us that story before?

SOPHIA Yes, but the last time it was Woolworth's, a toe nail clipper and John Cameron Swayze.

ACT ONE
Scene 2

LIVING ROOM – DAY
(*Blanche follows an exercise video on T.V. Dorothy watches*)

WOMAN'S VOICE (*From TV*) "Inhale . . . Good. Exhale and lean back. Hold the position. Keep breathing . . ."

DOROTHY The only time I get in a position like that is when I give birth.

BLANCHE Oww . . . my back.

DOROTHY   Blanche, are you all right?

BLANCHE   No. But I have to go on. No pain, no gain. I have to look good for Dirk. A man his age is used to a trim body with good tone.

DOROTHY   Then buy him a princess phone.
(Blanche takes pills)

DOROTHY   Now what are you doing?

BLANCHE   Taking my bee pollen, my sheep liver extract, and my fish oil protein. I'm getting years younger with each passing day.

DOROTHY   Fine, Blanche. When they defrost Walt Disney he'll have someone to go out with.

BLANCHE   Go ahead, make fun. But these treatments are working.

DOROTHY   Blanche, think for a minute. If you feel you have to put yourself through all this, what kind of relationship can this possibly be?

BLANCHE   A youthful relationship. A relationship I want. Dorothy, Dirk's the youngest man I've ever gone out with. If I'm going to keep him, I'm going to have to give it everything I've got. Now if you'll excuse me, I've got some road work to do.
(Blanche crosses to exit as Rose enters)

ROSE   Hi, Blanche. You look terrific.

BLANCHE   Thanks.
(Blanche exits)

ROSE   Blanche looks terrible.

DOROTHY   She looks terrible because all she eats is bee pollen.

ROSE   I know. Isn't it ironic that bees look so good.

DOROTHY   What are you doing home?

ROSE	I got off early to be with Mother.
DOROTHY	My mother took her to the track. *(Dorothy exits into kitchen. Rose follows)*

KITCHEN – CONTINUOUS

ROSE	You let her out of the house?
DOROTHY	No, Rose. She dug a tunnel out of her bedroom with a dessert spoon.
ROSE	Oh, my Lord. She's out on the street and it's almost dark.
DOROTHY	Rose, your mother's fine. She's with my mother.
ROSE	Sophia's different, Dorothy. She's . . . she's . . . she's your mother. My mother leads a very quiet life. All this excitement will be too much for her.
DOROTHY	Rose, she's betting on the horses, not rounding them up. *(Sophia and Alma enter)*
ALMA	*(Offstage)* Hello, anyone home. *(Sophia and Alma enter kitchen)*
ROSE	Mother, are you alright?
SOPHIA	She's fine. I'm fifty bucks in the hole.
ALMA	Look, Rosie, I won four hundred dollars!
DOROTHY	*(To Rose)* I told you there was nothing to worry about. *(Then)* Congratulations, Alma. Ma, I'll be in the living room when you're ready to explain where you got the fifty dollars you lost. *(Dorothy exits)*
ALMA	Sophia, how late is that mall open? I feel like

	getting wild. C'mon, I'll buy you some bikini underwear.
SOPHIA	Nah, they ride up on me. *(Sophia exits)*
ROSE	Mother, I think you've had enough for one day. Why don't you sit down and I'll bring you a nice cup of tea?
ALMA	I don't want to sit down. I want to go out and have some fun.
ROSE	Mother, you know how you get when you get tired. You're liable to lose your balance and break a hip. That's exactly how it happened last time.
ALMA	Rose, I broke my hip ice skating. I thought I could clear that fifth barrel.
ROSE	Do you want to go back in the hospital again? Did you have fun the last time?
ALMA	More fun than I'm having with you.
ROSE	Mother . . .
ALMA	Stop "Mothering" me. You're making me sorry I came. *(Alma exits to hallway)*

ACT ONE
Scene 3

LIVING ROOM – THE NEXT EVENING
(Rose looks out of the front door. Dorothy is grading papers)

| DOROTHY | Rose, you just checked the door two minutes ago. |
| ROSE | I thought I heard them. I should never have let |

them go shopping. It's too dangerous.

DOROTHY   What are you talking about?

ROSE   Just this morning I read that fourteen hundred people were injured in a food riot in Calcutta.

DOROTHY   (*Sarcastic*) Now you've got me worried.
(*Sophia enters*)

ROSE   Sophia, thank goodness you're home! Where's Mother?

SOPHIA   She was feeling lucky, so she wanted to try her hand at Jai Alai.

DOROTHY   Why didn't you go with her?

SOPHIA   I'm too short to play Jai Alai.

ROSE   Sophia, how could you leave my mother alone, roaming around in a strange city?

SOPHIA   Who's roaming? She's got a bus map, four hundred dollars and a Spanish-English dictionary.

ROSE   I can't believe my mother is riding around on a smelly old bus, being harrassed, pushed around, possibly even mugged by hostile teenagers with bad haircuts.

DOROTHY   Rose, listen to me. You're overreacting. Your mother is not a helpless child. She's an active, vital woman who can take care of herself.
PHONE RINGS

ROSE   I'll get that.
(*Rose answers*)
Hello. Yes, this is she. Oh, my Lord!

DOROTHY   Rose, what is it?

ROSE   (*Into phone*) Yes, I understand. I'll be right there.
(*Rose hangs up and grabs her keys*)

SOPHIA	Rose, what's wrong?
ROSE	That was the police.
DOROTHY	Is it your mother? Is she alright?
ROSE	She's fine. She's at the police station. They picked up my vital, active mother. She was lost and disoriented. What do you have to say to that?
DOROTHY	Rose, calm down.
ROSE	I have to go.
DOROTHY	I'll go with you.
ROSE	No thanks. You've been more than enough help already. *(Rose exits)*
DOROTHY	I hope Alma's alright.
SOPHIA	Don't worry about Alma. She's a tough old broad. *(Blanche enters)*
BLANCHE	Look at me, Dorothy. I have turned back the hands of time. Since Dirk asked me out I've dropped ten years. My face is smooth, my body's taut and my gears are grinding.
DOROTHY	Blanche, no matter what you do to your face, your body and your gears, you're still your age.
SOPHIA	Of course you are. Gravity always takes it toll. Look at me. I used to be a tall voluptuous blonde with a butt like granite.
BLANCHE	You think Dirk looks at me and sees an old woman? He sees a young, vibrant, passionate contemporary.
DOROTHY	Blanche, you haven't even been out with him yet.
BLANCHE	My instincts are infallible about this. Believe

me, I know men.

DOROTHY   No arguments here.
          DOORBELL

BLANCHE   (*Crossing to door*) A husband like Dirk could
          keep me young for another twenty years.

SOPHIA   Or kill you.
          (*Blanche opens door to Dirk*)

DIRK   You look gorgeous.

BLANCHE   Thank you. I haven't even had time to put on
          my make-up.
          (*Then*)
          Dirk, could you wait in your van for me? I'll be
          out in a minute.
          (*Dirk exits*)
          I do believe the man said "gorgeous". I'm gonna
          live forever.

DOROTHY   Not outside of an institution.
          (*Blanche laughs and exits*)
          END OF ACT ONE

ACT TWO
Scene 1

KITCHEN – LATER
(*Dorothy is stretched out under the kitchen sink tightening an
elbow joint with a wrench*)

SOPHIA   You almost finished?

DOROTHY   Yes, but I don't want to come out. This is the
          only peace and quiet I've had in two days.
          Blanche thinks she's Peter Pan, and Rose has
          turned into Mommie Dearest.
          (*Dorothy comes out from under the sink*)

SOPHIA	That's nothing. You think you're "Josephine The Plumber".
DOROTHY	I just saved us at least fifty dollars.
SOPHIA	Good. Between that and what I lost at the track you're even. *(Rose and Alma enter)*
ROSE	Mother, please.
ALMA	I told you, they had no right to take me in. I merely flagged down a policeman to ask for directions. Next thing I know, he's dragging me down to the station.
ROSE	He was just trying to help you, Mother.
ALMA	Then you had to come and scold me like a child in front of everyone.
ROSE	There's no point talking to you when you get like this. After a good night's sleep you won't be so cranky. We'll discuss this in the morning.
ALMA	I won't be here in the morning.
ROSE	What?
ALMA	I'm leaving early for Houston. I'm sure I'll have a much better time at your brother's. *(Alma exits to bedroom)*
SOPHIA	I'm gonna help her pack. Then I'll see if I can win some of that four hundred from her before she leaves. *(Sophia exits to bedroom)*
DOROTHY	*(Puts arm around Rose)* Rose, she's just angry. I'm sure she didn't mean that.
ROSE	How can she talk to me like that? I'm just trying to take care of her.
DOROTHY	Rose, can I say something? From one daughter to another. Remember back when we were

	teenagers? What was the one thing we wanted most from our mothers?
ROSE	A training bra?
DOROTHY	Alright, what was the second thing?
ROSE	Permission to shave our legs?
DOROTHY	Alright, no more question and answer. We wanted to be treated like adults. But as we get older we turn around and treat our mothers like little girls. Your mother wants to be treated like a woman. That's really not alot to ask. *(Rose considers a beat, then exits)*

ACT TWO
Scene 2

ROSE'S BEDROOM – CONTINUOUS
(Alma is packing. Sophia is cutting cards)

SOPHIA	Alright, I have a jack . . . *(Alma cuts cards. Then through gritted teeth)* . . . You have a queen. Okay I owe you forty bucks. *(Rose enters)*
ROSE	Sophia, will you excuse us?
SOPHIA	*(To Alma)* If I've got to leave now. I don't owe you anything.
ALMA	Who says?
SOPHIA	House rules.
ALMA	Okay. *(Sophia exits)*
ROSE	Mother? Am I really making you miserable?
ALMA	Yes, you are. I know you don't mean to, but you are.

ROSE   I'm sorry. Won't you stay and give me another chance?

ALMA   I don't know, Rosie.

ROSE   Please, Mother. I know I drive you crazy, but it's only because I love you.
(A beat)
You know, after Daddy died, I thought I'd never get over it. And Charlie. Well, not a day goes by when I don't think of him. And now that you're getting older, I'm afraid I'm going to lose you too. I guess that's why I fuss over you so much.

ALMA   I understand Rosie, but stopping me from living isn't going to stop me from dying.
(Alma holds out her arms for Rose. They hug warmly)

ROSE   *(Still hugging Alma)* I can't stand to think about it.

ALMA   Then don't. Let's just enjoy the time we have.

ACT TWO
Scene 3

KITCHEN – MOMENTS LATER
(Dorothy and Sophia are there)

DOROTHY   Ma, careful. That's my best china. You gave it to me on my wedding day, remember?

SOPHIA   Who could forget. I carried it all the way from Sicily. And for what? So you could get divorced. I should've gotten you something returnable. Like a donkey.

DOROTHY   I've eaten through a lot of good times on these plates.

SOPHIA	Yeah. You know, with Alma here, I've been thinking a lot about the two of us.
DOROTHY	You have?
SOPHIA	There's something I never told you. *(A beat)* You do a lot of things wrong.
DOROTHY	Thanks, Ma. So do you.
SOPHIA	But one thing you never do is treat me like an old lady, you treat me like a person. I appreciate that. You're a good daughter, Dorothy.
DOROTHY	I'm overwhelmed, Ma. I don't know what to say.
SOPHIA	You know what you could say. You could say I don't owe you the fifty bucks.
DOROTHY	You're a crazy lady. I love you. *(Dorothy kisses Sophia on cheek)*
SOPHIA	I love you, too, pussycat.

ACT TWO
Scene 4

RESTAURANT – NIGHT
(Blanche, Dirk and a waiter are there)

BLANCHE	I believe I'll have the escargot, the duck a l'orange and a tossed salad with blue cheese dressing.
DIRK	I'll have the watercress salad with two lemon wedges.
BLANCHE	That sounds great! I didn't see that on my menu. *(Dirk shows it to Blanche)*

I'll have the same thing.
(Waiter takes menus and exits)

BLANCHE   Isn't this place lovely? It's one of my favourite restaurants.

DIRK   I'm into macrobiotics myself.

BLANCHE   Oh, me too. I just like the atmosphere. Sometimes I bring macrobiotic take-out food and eat it here.

DIRK   Yeah. Wow.

BLANCHE   So, Dirk. What did you do before you got into teaching aerobics?

DIRK   I worked at a museum.

BLANCHE   You're kidding! I work at a museum. I love art.

DIRK   Me too, I love lifting it.

BLANCHE   I beg your pardon?

DIRK   I used to unload the trucks. I don't know why but lifting those statues really helped define my deltoids.
(Dirk lifts table)

BLANCHE   Yes. Isn't that fascinating. Put that down, honey.
(Dirk sets table down)
So, Dirk, have you read any good books lately?

DIRK   Pumping Iron. I saw the movie, too. I don't think it did the book justice.

BLANCHE   How could it?

DIRK   I really like being with you.

BLANCHE   Why thank you, Dirk.

DIRK   I like the way you sound, the way you look.

BLANCHE   Why thank you, Dirk.

DIRK   You remind me of my mother. She lives in

Seattle, and I haven't seen her in three years. But when I'm with you, I kind of feel like I'm home, with Mom.

BLANCHE   Waiter?
(Waiter crosses to table)
Eighty-six the watercress. I'll have the duck and a double Jack Daniels on the rocks.
(Waiter exits)
So, Dirk. What else have you lifted lately?

ACT TWO
Scene 5

KITCHEN – NIGHT

(Rose and Dorothy are washing and drying the dishes. Sophia and Alma are seated at the kitchen table, playing black-jack. Alma has just won a pot of 4 pretzel sticks to add to her pile on the table)

SOPHIA   Come on, one more hand.

ALMA   I'm a little tired, Sophia. I'd like to cash in. Let's see . . . these are worth a dollar a piece? I must have twenty or thirty pretzel sticks.
(Sophia crushes pretzel sticks with her fist)

SOPHIA   Now you've got pretzel dust.

DOROTHY   Ma, don't be a sore loser. You owe her thirty dollars.

SOPHIA   You're absolutely right, Dorothy. I stand corrected. Pay her.

ROSE   Gee, it's getting late. I wonder how Blanche's date is going.

DOROTHY   I'm a little worried.

ROSE   Me too. I feel uncomfortable with her dating a younger man.

DOROTHY   I'm not concerned about her dating a younger man. It's just that her expectations are so high.

ROSE   You mean you approve?

DOROTHY   Why not? What's so terrible? I did it once.

ROSE   *(Shocked)* You? You dated a younger man?

DOROTHY   Yes, Rose. It was before I had the hump on my back. When Stan and I split up, I went back to school for my teaching certificate and I met this handsome young education student from Saudi Arabia. We studied together and eventually started dating. I introduced him to baseball and Barbara Streisand. He introduced me to couscous and some things that are none of your business. It was very nice while it lasted.

ALMA   Personally, I don't see anything wrong with dating a younger man. The three years I spent with Ben were some of the happiest in my life.

ROSE   *(Incredulous)* Mother!

ALMA   After Daddy passed on, and you kids moved out, there was no way I could handle the place by myself. So I hired a farm hand. He was such a nice young man. Raved about my cooking. I guess they didn't feed him very well in prison. *(Rose reacts)*
Anyway, we really enjoyed being with each other. It was an especially lonely time for me and it was nice to have someone to talk to. After a while, he moved in. I would never have gotten through those years without Ben. When it was over, it was over. We were both better off for having known each other.

ROSE   Mother, how could you? A drifter, an ex-con . . .

   (Alma glares at Rose)

	I'm sorry. You said he made you happy. That's what matters. I'm sure he was very nice for a drifting ex-con . . .
ALMA	Thank you, Rosie. I think I'm going to turn in now. Goodnight.
SOPHIA	I'll go with you. I'll bring the cards. (*Grabs cards*) Can I ask you a personal question, Alma? Did this Ben teach you how to gamble?
ALMA	Yep. Taught me how to play cards and carve a pistol out of soap. (*Sophia tosses cards back on table. She and Alma exit*)
ROSE	You think our kids will want us around when we're their age?
DOROTHY	Rose, they don't want us to know. (*Blanche enters, agitated*) Blanche.
BLANCHE	I don't want to talk about it.
DOROTHY	What's the matter? What happened?
BLANCHE	My date with Dirk was a disaster. He was looking for a mother, not a lover. It was humiliating.
ROSE	I think it's sweet.
BLANCHE	You would, Betty Crocker. (*Then*) I'm sorry, Rose. I'm just really depressed. For the first time in my life I feel over forty.
DOROTHY	Do you know why that is, honey?
BLANCHE	Why?
DOROTHY	Because you're over fifty.
BLANCHE	Don't I know it. Over fifty and over-the-hill.

DOROTHY   Blanche, age is nothing but a state of mind.

BLANCHE   Tell that to my thighs. I just want to die. I can't stand it. I can't stand it.

DOROTHY   Neither can I. You have your looks, your health, a few bucks in the bank and friends who love you. That's a hell of a lot more than most people have. I'm not going to stay here one second longer and listen to you feel sorry for yourself . . . and neither is Rose.

ROSE   Yeah.
           (Dorothy grabs Rose and exits. For a second, Blanche is in shock, thinking about what Dorothy has said. Slowly, a smile spreads across her face)
           END OF ACT TWO

Love Under The Big Top

Written by: Tracy Gamble &
Richard Vaczy
Directed by: Terry Hughes

· *Introduction* ·

WRITERS Tracy Gamble and Richard Vaczy manage to seamlessly bolt together the injustices of the legal system, concern for the environment, career-switching in later life and the problems of mature romance without ever force-fitting the various component parts.

Rose, normally content with cosy domesticity, is galvanized into saving the dolphin after she and Blanche have enjoyed a boat trip. For once, placing her sweetness-and-light demeanour on the back burner, she spits out her new commitment:

"Wonderful, my foot. Blanche, you saw that dolphin. All tangled up in that tuna boat's net. Thousands of them die that way each year. We have to do something."

In an episode which typifies the tendency of American television to showcase liberal concerns on primetime TV (see Lou Grant for further details), Blanche, also joining the Friends of Sea Mammals, accompanies Rose on her protest. Thus the two characters who normally engage in nothing more than sentiment (Rose) or sex (Blanche) go down to the docks to breathe hellfire on the tuna fishermen.

Yet, in order to lace the political punch with some gutsy humour, Blanche has to be egged on just a little:

"I didn't expect to be carrying picket signs on some grungy dock. I was hoping more for a fund-raiser cocktail party. With Chinese lanterns and Portuguese ...no Hispanic ...waiters in tight black pants. And we hire a band to play fish songs in pirate suits with muscles bulging . . ."

Sophia also lightens this scene by describing her own boat trip to America as a young immigrant. The "tired, poor huddled mass eating marinara sauce out of a can", who spent their time pinning the tail on the French, also had to suffer "some guy from Palemo [who] forgot his accordion so he sat around singing 'O Solo Mio' while squeezing a monkey."

Dorothy, meanwhile, is fretting about her burgeoning romance with Ken, "one of Miami's most successful lawyers", since, tired of being a lawyer, he wants to make a complete professional volte-face and re-emerge as a circus clown.

Ken is the source of much fun ("Dorothy, you know you have the most beautiful eyes? And a quarter in your ear?"), but he also represents an idealized lawyer who refuses to continue cooperating as a well-oiled cog in a gilded system. Confessing just "how little my job actually had to do with justice", he also adds that his youthful, rosy view of law has been tainted:

"I went to law school so I could fight for the little guy. Now I am fighting for multinational corporations."

Believing that he "can contribute more to the world in big red shoes", he does, however, make one final appearance in court when he arrives as the righteous avenger to steer Blanche and Rose clear of dophin trouble.

The exuberant proof that both late-life romance and career change are possible, he appears in an episode which for once moves outside the Golden Girls' home to both courtroom and dock.

CAST

DOROTHY, ROSE, BLANCHE, SOPHIA, KEN, JUDGE,
FISHERMAN.

ACT ONE
Scene 1

LIVING ROOM – EARLY EVENING
(Sophia enters, sits. Blanche enters front door with sailing gear)

BLANCHE	Hi, Sophia. Boy, I tell you, there is nothing more invigorating than spending a little time on a boat.
SOPHIA	Oh yeah? Not when I sailed to America. Picture it. There we were – a tired, poor, huddled mass eating marinara sauce out of a can. It was hell. And the entertainment. Some guy from Palermo forgot his accordion so he sat around singing "O Solo Mio" while squeezing a monkey. *(Blanche laughs)*
BLANCHE	Sophia.
SOPHIA	Sophia what? It was the worst time of my life. If it weren't for "pin-the-tail-on-the-French", we would've gone stir-crazy. *(Rose enters with sailing gear*
ROSE	Hi, Sophia.
BLANCHE	Rose, I was just telling Sophia what a wonderful day we had.
ROSE	Wonderful, my foot. Blanche, you saw that dolphin. All tangled up in that tuna boat's net. Thousands of them die that way each year. We have to do something.

BLANCHE	You are absolutely right. From this moment on, no more tuna fish.
ROSE	Blanche, you hate tuna fish.
BLANCHE	All right then. No more tuna fishermen. *(Dorothy enters, dressed to the nines)*
DOROTHY	Hi, girls. Do these pearls look okay with this?
BLANCHE	Honey pearls look fine with everything from the fanciest dress to . . . that. You have another date with Ken. Oh, Sophia, do you believe it?
SOPHIA	And I thought my head was spinning from the splash of vino in my lemonade.
ROSE	Sophia, you don't put wine in your lemonade.
SOPHIA	No. You're right. I don't. It was a joke. Ha. Ha.
BLANCHE	Your Ken is quite a catch, Dorothy. For once I'm a bit jealous.
SOPHIA	What's not to be jealous about? The man's gorgeous. He's got money and class. I couldn't be happier for you, Dorothy. I just want to give you a loving mother's advice – *don't blow it!*
DOROTHY	Ma, I have no intention of blowing this. No, Ken is . . . perfect. I mean aside from being one of Miami's most successful lawyers . . . *(Sophia knocks on wood)* Thank you, Ma. The man is caring, he's sensitive. Do you know that on weekends he actually puts on a clown's costume and entertains sick kids at the hospital? *DOORBELL* I mean, what more could I want from a man? Get it out of the gutter, Blanche. *(Dorothy primps, opens door. It's Ken Whittingham)*
KEN	Dorothy.

DOROTHY	Hi, sweetheart. How was your day?
KEN	Well, my ulcer didn't flare up and I'm having dinner with you. So I guess it's perfect. *(Ken, Sophia and Blanche, simultaneously)*
SOPHIA	Hi.
KEN	Hi
BLANCHE	Hi, Ken. *(Then)*
SOPHIA	Hey, Kenny. What's a nice boy like you doing with ulcers anyway? You got a job that pays and a girl who'll do anything for you. Anything. You will, won't you, Dorothy?
DOROTHY	I'll take that as a "Have a good time."
KEN	Don't worry, Mrs Petrillo, I'll have your little girl home at a reasonable hour.
SOPHIA	Don't bother. You kids have fun. I won't wait up. Have her back by Tuesday, no questions asked. *(Dorothy and Ken exit)* She's gonna blow it.

ACT ONE
Scene 2

KITCHEN — DAY (A FEW DAYS LATER)
(Rose on phone. Blanche licks envelopes)

ROSE	Okay, Paul, we'll see you at the rally on pier five. Oh, the dolphin will really appreciate it. *(Hangs up)* Oh, isn't this exciting? Taking part in a protest. Standing up as free Americans and exercising our right to say, "We're mad as hell and we're not going to take it anymore!"

BLANCHE	I'm out of spit. Can I go now?
ROSE	Twenty envelopes and you're ready to quit? Blanche, we joined the Friends of Sea Mammals for a reason. You are so unmotivated.
BLANCHE	Well, when I joined this Mammals With Blowholes thing, I didn't expect to be carrying picket signs on some grungy dock. I was hoping more for a fund-raiser cocktail party. With Chinese lanterns and Portuguese – no, Hispanic – waiters in tight black pants. And we hire a band to play fish songs in pirate suits with muscles bulging . . .
ROSE	Your mouth is watering now, Blanche. Keep licking. *(Sophia and Dorothy enter with groceries)*
DOROTHY	Hi, girls.
BLANCHE	You two are back early.
SOPHIA	Of course we're back early. Ken called before. He says he needs to talk to Dorothy about something "very important".
ROSE	Dorothy!
BLANCHE	My God, Dorothy, he's going to pop the question.
DOROTHY	Oh, I don't know that.
BLANCHE	Of course you do. What else could it be? Oh, honey, congratulations.
DOROTHY	Eh, you're more excited than I am.
BLANCHE	Well, why not, Dorothy? Just think of it. Life with a successful attorney. The summer homes, the glamorous social circles, those impulsive little trips to Europe with rascally Romans pinching your bottom. You're a lucky girl, Dorothy. I hate you.

DOROTHY   Oh, this is just crazy talk. I mean, we've only
                been seeing each other for three months. I've
                never even thought of what it would be like if I
                were . . .
                (Dreamy)
                . . .Mrs. Kenneth Whittingham . . .

SOPHIA   Has a nice ring to it.
                DOORBELL
                Go get 'em, pussycat. Just remember, you and I
                come as a package.

DOROTHY   Maaa . . .

ACT ONE
Scene 3

LIVING ROOM – DAY (CONTINUOUS)
(Dorothy opens door. It's Ken)

KEN   Hi.
                (They kiss)
                Sweetheart, I am so excited.

DOROTHY   Oh?

KEN   It's just that I've come to a major decision.

DOROTHY   Oh?

KEN   And it's a decision that affects both of us.

DOROTHY   Ooooh?

KEN   Sit down. Close your eyes and I'll give you a
                hint.

DOROTHY   Okey-dokey.
                (Dorothy closes eyes, extends ring finger, waits.
                Ken places red ball on his nose)

KEN   Well?
                (Dorothy opens eyes)
                Can you guess what my decision is?

DOROTHY	You're becoming Irish?
KEN	No. I'm becoming a clown. A full-time circus clown.
DOROTHY	Ken, isn't this a bit sudden? Odd and a bit sudden?
KEN	No. I've been doing it for years at children's hospitals. S'been the one bright spot in my life. That and you. Dorothy, I've been lawyering seventy hours a week since I was twenty-five. Can change a man.
DOROTHY	Yeah, but you're so successful.
KEN	I'm also sixty and I'm miserable. Ah, I went to law school so I could fight for the little guy. Now I'm fighting for multinational corporations. I'm so frazzled, I find myself sneaking into the washroom to make balloon giraffes. Dorothy, I really need for you to understand this. I've been thinking a lot lately. I think we're in this for the long haul. Dorothy, I think this is going to be a very serious relationship. *(They lean in to kiss)*
DOROTHY	I feel like a virgin. Where do the noses go?
KEN	I'm sorry. *(He takes ball off nose and gives her a small kiss)* What do you say? You with me?
DOROTHY	Of course.
KEN	Oh great. *(Dorothy sighs)* Then how about a celebration? I'm having dinner with some new friends from the circus. Join me?
DOROTHY	Might as well get my feet wet. *(Grabs sweater, they start to exit)*

Oh, uh, Ken. There won't be, like, a-a dozen tiny dogs, hopping on hind legs, wearing funny hats?

KEN   Ho-ho, I wish.
(They exit)

ACT ONE
Scene 4

LIVING ROOM – NEXT DAY
(Dorothy and Blanche enter from kitchen)

BLANCHE   Oh come on, tell me. How big a disaster was last night?

DOROTHY   It wasn't a disaster, Blanche. It was just uncomfortable. No, I tried to find some common ground, something I could talk to Ken's circus friends about. But it turns out "The Human Cannonball" doesn't do that much reading.

BLANCHE   Does Ken know how you feel?

DOROTHY   He asked me how I felt, if I had a good time, and I had to tell him the truth. I just didn't fit in with the other clowns' wives.
(Rose enters)

ROSE   Dorothy, I've been thinking. It might help you get your mind off this Ken thing for awhile. Why don't you join us at the rally?

DOROTHY   Oh no, Rose, I don't think I . . .

BLANCHE   *(Overlapping Dorothy)* Oh yeah, Dorothy, oh do. Oh, get out of yourself. It's for a noble cause. Or are you so self-centred that you'd rather wallow in self-pity?

DOROTHY   You're right. I'll do it.

BLANCHE   Oh good. Rose, Dorothy's taking my place.
          (Sophia enters)

SOPHIA   There you are, pussycat. What's this news
          about Ken? He gave you a ring, didn't he?

BLANCHE   Yeah. Three of them.

DOROTHY   Look, Ma, I don't know how to say this. So I'll
          just give it to you straight out. Ken is becoming
          a clown.

SOPHIA   *(After a beat)* Scusi?

DOROTHY   Ma. He's tired of being a lawyer so he's joining
          the circus.

SOPHIA   What did you do to him?!

DOROTHY   I didn't do anything.

SOPHIA   Yeah, right. One day the man's a lawyer, the
          next he's clown. Perfectly natural.

DOROTHY   Ma, please, this is hard enough as it is.

SOPHIA   Oh, I'm sorry, sweetheart. I just tend to get a
          little upset when people *ruin my life!*

ROSE   Sophia, I don't know what all the hullabaloo is
          about. Dating a circus clown would be a dream
          come true for me.

BLANCHE   Reach for the stars, Rose.

ROSE   No, it would. Think about it. Seeing him push
          those little pigs around in a baby carriage.
          Getting hit with a bucket of confetti any time
          you want. And sitting up there in the stands,
          watching him sweep that spotlight into a little
          circle and thinking – that's my man!

DOROTHY   Oh, why did this have to happen? Just when I
          meet someone that I-I feel I have a future with,
          Ken does this. I mean, I know I should be more
          supportive, but the fact is, I'm embarrassed.

ROSE   Don't be ridiculous, Dorothy. You love the man for who he is. It's not like he's driving you around in a tiny car with a giant key on the back. Is he?
SFX: Doorbell
(Dorothy answers, it's Ken)

KEN   Hi, sweetheart.

DOROTHY   You are driving the Lincoln tonight, aren't you?

KEN   Sure. Oh, two things. We're, uh, doubling with Phil and Nancy tonight. Two things you have to remember. Call them "little people" and they hate to be patted on the head. I found out the hard way.

SOPHIA   Kenny. Come here. What's with this clown business? Couldn't you be a lawyer and just hang out with clowns?

KEN   Oh, I know it sounds a little odd, Mrs. Petrillo, but right now I'm just burned out on law. Frankly, at this point, I think I can contribute more to the world in big red shoes and a spinning bow tie and carrying a little umbrella that rains on me.

SOPHIA   I see.
(Beat)
Dorothy? Eh – *(She ushers Dorothy out front door)*

SOPHIA   (O.C) What did you do to him?!
END OF ACT ONE

ACT TWO
Scene 1

DOCKSIDE – NEXT DAY
(Rose with megaphone gives speech to demonstrators, who march by gateway of fence that leads to tuna boats. Dorothy and Blanche are there with picket signs)

ROSE   *(Into megaphone)* We may not agree with the fishermen, but we want this demonstration to be peaceful. In the tradition of . . . you know, the short, bald, Indian fellow with glasses and the diaper . . . you know, the one who didn't eat and won an Oscar . . .

BLANCHE   Your sign's drooping again, Dorothy. Now what's the matter?

DOROTHY   It's Ken. I don't know which end is up. He called me this morning. He wants me to travel with the circus. I'm afraid we're gonna have to call it quits.

BLANCHE   Oh, honey, I'd think twice before I cut that guy off. At your age, how many chances at the brass ring do you have left?

ROSE   *(Into megaphone)* All creatures must learn to coexist. Back where I come from, they do. That's why the brown bear and the field mouse can share their lives and live in harmony. 'Course, they can't mate or the mice would explode. You know what I mean.

DOROTHY   I think Rose needs to work on her metaphors.

BLANCHE   Listen, honey, I know you're down in the dumps, but I'm so glad you came. I really want us to make a difference today.

DOROTHY   Oh, Blanche, I am impressed. You have really changed your tune.

BLANCHE   You know, it's funny how that happened. There I was, staying up last night coming up with excuses to get out of this and then it occurred to me: I said, "Water Lily," – that's what I call myself sometimes – "Water Lily, you've never done anything like this in your life. Now this is important. For the love of Mother Earth and the love of Mother Nature, commit yourself to this, Blanche Devereaux!" Isn't that exciting?

DOROTHY   Caught a rerun of "Flipper" on cable, did you?

BLANCHE   A particularly touching one. Where Flipper comes to the rescue. It was only after that I picked up Rose's pamphlets and read about these magnificent creatures.

DOROTHY   Oh, that's beautiful . . . Water Lily?

BLANCHE   Uh-huh.
(*A fisherman approaches Rose*)

FISHERMAN   All right, you dolphin people, get away from the gate.

BLANCHE   Watch it. What're you . . .

ROSE   Why can't you people see the light?

FISHERMAN   Why can't you people see that there's another point of view?
(*Takes Rose by the arm, starts to pull at her*)
Now get away from here, we've got work to do.

ROSE   You take your hands off me . . .!

BLANCHE   (*Lunging at fisherman holding Rose*) You let her go!
(*Blanche throws a punch. Fisherman is down. Ladies and crowd react, all talking and shouting at once*)

BLANCHE: 'For the love of Mother Earth and the love of
Mother Nature, commit yourself to this,
Blanche Devereaux!'

ROSE: Honey, you can't change the world in one day.

KEN: If the circus is ever in town, I'll leave the tent flap open for you.

Not Another Monday

SOPHIA: If my heart stopped beating, I'd want every doctor in town jumping up and down on my chest.

BLANCHE: We could change its diaper and see if it has a winkie.

SOPHIA: You can still be homecoming queen. It'll just be
           a different kind of home.

DOROTHY: (*on stage*) That's my mother. The incredible
shrinking woman.

BLANCHE: Did you really think this was gonna be a story about sex? This is a beautiful Christmas story, Dorothy.

DOROTHY: Oh, you could charm the pants off anybody.
I have to believe that. Otherwise, I was easy.

SOPHIA: We have each other. There's always someone
            there.

ROSE: Well, maybe she had trouble with her
          pacemaker.

BLANCHE: I've had a life-altering experience, Simon.
I need time to think.

ROSE: I haven't been this scared since 1952 when St.
          Olaf's most active volcano threatened to erupt.

ROSE: Damn it, why is this happening to me? I mean, this isn't supposed to happen to people like me.

DOROTHY: The last thing my mother said to me was that she wanted me to keep my feet on the floor.

SOPHIA: Pussycat, you're never too old to make a fool of yourself.

ACT TWO
Scene 2

(COURTROOM – LATER THAT DAY
(Blanche, Rose and Dorothy sit with other protesters in spectator area, guarded by bailiff. Sophia enters and hurries over to Dorothy)

SOPHIA	Sweetheart, I came as soon as I could.
DOROTHY	Things got out of hand down at the dock. I'm fine.
SOPHIA	Don't worry. I called Ken, he's parking the car.
DOROTHY	*(To the ladies)* Oh, did you hear that? Did you hear that? Ken is going to save us. *(To fellow demonstrators)* Everybody, did you hear that? We'll be out of here in no time. My mother called my boyfriend, a top Miami lawyer. Nothing to worry about. We are in good hands. *(Enter Ken in full clown attire, suit on hanger. His huge clown shoes slap ground as he walks)*
KEN	Oh, Dorothy, sweetheart, there you are.
DOROTHY	My God! Ma, you didn't tell me he was in a clown suit!
SOPHIA	Oh yeah.
DOROTHY	Ken, how could you . . .?
KEN	Sophia called me at rehearsal. I'll change. I just wanted to make sure you were all right.
DOROTHY	Oh . . . *(Hugs her)* CLOWN HORN
JUDGE	Is counsel for the demonstrators present?
KEN	Here, Your Honour.

· 97 ·

DOROTHY   Oh God.

JUDGE   Will the clown approach the bench?

KEN   Dorothy, I can do this.

DOROTHY   Can you do it without the nose?

KEN   Yes.
(He takes ball off nose and approaches)

JUDGE   *(To Ken)* What the hell are you trying to do?

KEN   Your Honour, I know this looks a little odd.
But I am a registered member of the Bar. I have
a, uh, card here to prove it.
*(Empties pockets: rubber chicken, horn, foam
mallet, dove feathers, etc.)*

DOROTHY   We're going to jail.

JUDGE   I believe you, counsellor, I believe you. Just –
just proceed.

KEN   Thank you, Your Honour.

JUDGE   Make it quick.

KEN   Your Honour, uh, this may be my very last
appearance before the bar, would you, uh,
indulge me just a little? Thank you. You know,
I have been practicing law for many, many
years, and it's always amazed me how little my
job actually had to do with justice.
(Aside)
This stuff sounds a little better when you've got
lapels and a vest.
(Then, continuing)
Anyway, my clients are charged with trespass.
But the only real crime they committed was
their overzealous championing of the
defenseless dolphin. The dolphin, Your
Honour, that for centuries has rescued men lost
at sea . . .guided ships back to port. No, my

clients were not trespassing. My clients were returning the favour. They simply wanted to protect some of nature's best creations from extinction. Your Honour, you have the opportunity today to make a very disillusioned lawyer happy. Please answer to a law higher than this state's and dispense some real justice here.
(*Courtroom bursts into applause*)

JUDGE   (*Bangs gavel*) Please, let's have a little quiet here. That was a great speech.

KEN   Thank you, Your Honour.

JUDGE   But, uh, help me out here. How 'bout something from a law book?

KEN   Okay. The fracas occurred on a seaside dock abutting navigable waters. I don't believe that this court has any jurisdiction.

JUDGE   That sounds legal to me. Counsellor, your last day has been a good one.
(*Bangs gavel once*)
Case dismissed.
(*Crowd stands, celebrates. Dorothy hugs Ken*)

ACT TWO
Scene 3

LIVING ROOM – LATER THAT DAY
(*Rose, Blanche and Sophia enter*)

SOPHIA   I want you two jailbirds to feel at home. Dinner's at six. Pass it on.
(*She exits to kitchen*)

BLANCHE   Rose, honey, what is the matter?

ROSE   We didn't accomplish anything today,

Blanche. Those tuna fishermen are gonna be right out there again tomorrow doing the same thing. I swear, I feel like a failure.

BLANCHE Honey, you can't change the world in one day. But just think about what we did do. I bet we saved a few dolphin by keeping that boat off the water and the next time you're walking along the beach and you see a school swim by, why you can think, "Maybe I saved those gorgeous creatures from those horrible nets." You still think we were a failure?

ROSE You're right. I just wish we could save 'em all.

BLANCHE You wanna do more? Fine. Let's go back down to the dock.

ROSE Really?

BLANCHE Sure. I know a waterfront bar where a lot of foreign fishermen hang out.

ROSE Do you think they'd be willing to listen to me?

BLANCHE Well sure they will, honey. They don't speak English and they're horny.
(*They exit front door as Dorothy and Ken enter. Ken still in clown garb, minus makeup, wearing overcoat*)

DOROTHY Ah, where're you going?
(*They answer simultaneously*)

ROSE To demonstrate.

BLANCHE To celebrate.
(*Rose and Blanche exit*)

KEN So, anything special you want to do tonight?

DOROTHY Ken, there is something . . .

KEN Dorothy, you know you have the most beautiful eyes? And a quarter in your ear?
(*He pulls quarter from behind her ear*)

DOROTHY	Ken, we really have to talk.
KEN	What's the matter, sweetheart?
DOROTHY	I don't know whether this is harder to say or harder to hear. Ken, you're a loveable man, with a lot of loveable qualities, but . . . I don't love you.
KEN	It's this clown thing, isn't it?
DOROTHY	I thought that's what was bothering me. But, Ken, if I loved you, I'd follow you anywhere. I'm sorry.
KEN	I see.
DOROTHY	I think we were both trying too hard to make this work. You on your terms, me on mine. But I know that I am not prepared to give up my life. And, Ken, could you give up the circus for me? Could you give up the laughter? The smiles on those children's faces?
KEN	D'you know something, Dorothy, I don't think I could. Could I give up the fat lady for you? No. Could I give up the elephants for you? No. The chimps? The sword-swallower – ?
DOROTHY	Ken –
KEN	The, the –
DOROTHY	I think I have a grip on this.
KEN	I guess at our age, we do a lot of wishful thinking.
DOROTHY	We did come close, though.
KEN	If the circus is ever in town, I'll leave the tent flap open for you.
DOROTHY	I'm gonna miss you. (*They hug. Dorothy takes hankie from Ken's overcoat to wipe away a tear, moves away and*

*takes a clothesline of handkerchiefs in tow. She
reacts, shakes head with a laugh, then hugs Ken.*
END OF ACT TWO

NOT ANOTHER MONDAY

Written by: GAIL PARENT
Directed by: TERRY HUGHES

· Introduction ·

THE WRITER OF THIS EPISODE, Gail Parent, follows the typical Golden Girls mix of problem scenarios and lively fun, yet never lets weighty matters put a brake on the crackerjack pace.

Two heavyweight issues, the meaning of life in one's final years and the right to take that life oneself, gallop towards Sophia, the only Golden Girl of the group who normally dismisses everything with a quick barb.

Having been introduced to Sophia's friend Martha, after they've returned from the funeral of a mutual friend, Lydia, ("the guest of honour had lipstick on her teeth and didn't give a damn"), we next witness an apparently hearty Martha as she packs down a cholesterol-heavy restaurant dinner and several Harvey Wallbangers.

Confessing that she suffers from many ailments, including arthritis, high blood pressure and angina, she invites Sophia to her house the next day, while declaring to her astonished friend:

"I want you to be there when I kill myself."

Bringing a heavy emotional rush to the proceedings, and making the customary cheery banter seem as if it comes from Mars, Martha explains to Sophia in an unhysterical, matter-of-fact manner:

"You don't understand. I'm afraid of the pain, of the hurting. I'm afraid of being alone. Of dying alone. I can take the pills myself. But I want you to be there and hold my hand."

Embodying the anxiety of many old people, she later

admits that, "I don't have the courage to die by inches." Envious of Sophia's community life ("you live with friends and family . . . holidays and warmth. I hear the silence"), she extracts patience, consideration and compassion from a Sophia who usually hides all three under a crisp volley of put-downs.

As ever, sparkling humour is never far off. Pulling back from Martha's tortured introspection, the camera homes in on Blanche who reveals her own unique scale of prioritites:

"When my time comes, I sure want somebody to put me out of my misery if something tragic happens, like I get a fatal illness or I've lost my looks."

Forming a nice counterpoint to Martha's gloomy world view is the arrival of a friend's baby whose sudden high temperature causes concern for his welfare. The introduction of the baby is also a successful attempt to form a startling comic contrast to the scenes with Martha. So, while Rose practices changing diapers on a turkey, Blanche tarts herself up for the local doctor.

Blanche: "How do I look?"

Dorothy: "It's all wrong, Blanche. The baby doesn't match your shoes."

CAST

DOROTHY, ROSE, BLANCHE, SOPHIA, HARRY, MARTHA
LAMONT, YOUNG WOMAN, YOUNG MAN, MAITRE D',
BARTENDER.

ACT ONE
Scene 1

KITCHEN – AFTERNOON
*(Rose diapers turkey. Blanche and Dorothy enter front with
groceries)*

DOROTHY	Rose, what are you doing?
ROSE	I'm diapering a turkey. It's been so long since I changed a diaper, I figured I'd practice before the baby gets here. *(Sophia and Martha enter, dressed in black. Ad-lib hellos)*
DOROTHY	Ma. Hello, Martha. Where were you?
SOPHIA	I'll give you a hint. The guest of honour had lipstick on her teeth and didn't give a damn.
BLANCHE	Who died?
MARTHA	My best friend, Lydia.
DOROTHY	I'm so sorry.
MARTHA	She suffered so. It was a blessing in disguise.
SOPHIA	I always wondered why blessings wore disguises. If I were a blessing I'd run around naked. DOORBELL
ROSE	Oh, that must be the baby!
SOPHIA	There's a baby coming?
ROSE	A couple from my church are going camping over the weekend and we get to take care of the baby.

SOPHIA   Good. Maybe now you'll get some food I can
          chew.
          (*Blanche, Rose and Dorothy exit to living room*)
          How about a cup of tea, Martha?

MARTHA   A little. I made a pig of myself at the funeral.

SOPHIA   It was nice. Everybody had a good time.

MARTHA   I'm going to miss her so much.

SOPHIA   I know, but you said yourself, the last few weeks
          were so hard on her. At least now she's resting
          peacefully.

MARTHA   I feel so bad.

SOPHIA   Hey, I'm the one who should feel bad. Lydia
          and I were wearing the same dress.

ACT ONE
Scene 2

LIVING ROOM – AFTERNOON (CONTINUOUS)
(*Young couple there with Dorothy, Blanche and Rose. Baby in
carriage, diaper bag hangs on it*)

YOUNG   Honey, can we go now? I've been planning this
MAN   for months. A weekend alone in the woods. It's
          gonna be perfect.

ROSE   Oh, it sound romantic. Maybe you'll have
          another baby.

YOUNG   I'd better make sure we packed everything.
MAN   (*He exits*)

YOUNG   Well, thanks again. Goodbye, Francis. You be
WOMAN   good now.
          (*Rose accompanies young woman to door*)

ROSE   Now don't you worry about a thing. You go and
          have a good time.

(Young woman exits, Rose closes door. Dorothy and Blanche look at baby in carriage)

BLANCHE   What a beautiful little thing.

DOROTHY   Oh, yes. What is it, Rose, a boy or a girl?

ROSE   Of course.

DOROTHY   I mean, is it Frances as in Francie, or Francis as in Frank?

ROSE   I don't know. It's wearing yellow.

DOROTHY   We could find out, Rose.

ROSE   How?

DOROTHY   Put on the Dolphins game and see if it watches . . . By looking, Rose!

BLANCHE   We could change its diaper and see if it has a winkie.

DOROTHY   A winkie?

BLANCHE   That's the scientific term for it when it's little. *(Rose feels around in carriage)*

ROSE   But the baby isn't wet. *(Blanche hands cloth diaper to Dorothy)*

BLANCHE   Well, we'll change it anyway. Here you go.

DOROTHY   Here *I* go?

BLANCHE   The best time to change a diaper is when there's nothing in it.

ROSE   I'll do it. You can help me. Okay, ready? One, two, three! *(She takes off diaper)* BRIEF STREAM OF WATER RISES FROM CARRIAGE *(They step back)*

BLANCHE/   Frank.
ROSE/
DOROTHY

ACT ONE
Scene 3

LE MARMITON RESTAURANT – FOLLOWING NIGHT
(Sophia, in her best dress, enters)

MAITRE D' May I help you, madam?

SOPHIA How do you know I'm not a mademoiselle?

MAITRE D' Because what man in his right mind would
leave you to languish on the vine?
(He kisses her hand)

SOPHIA If this was Sicily, you wouldn't have any lips
left. Take me to my friend Martha Lamont's
table and try not to fall in love.

MAITRE D' Miss Lamont is waiting for you at the bar.

SOPHIA Oh, good. With luck she found somebody
who'll pay for dinner.
(Maitre D' leads Sophia to bar where Martha sits)
Martha, you look terrific! Are those new
knee-highs?

MARTHA It's a new attitude. Eat, drink and be merry.
*(Sophia tries to get up on bar stool, but it's too high.
She gestures for Maitre D')*

SOPHIA Hey, Jacques, give me a hand and watch where
you put it.
*(Maitre D' comes over. Sophia raises arms. Maitre
D' lifts her onto stool)*
That was better than I thought it would be.
Now I can't wait to get down.
(Maitre D' exits. Bartender approaches)

BARTENDER Hi. Can I get you ladies drinks?

SOPHIA I'll have a Manhattan, and I'm watching, so
don't slip me any of the cheap stuff.

MARTHA I'll have another Harvey Wallbanger.

(Bartender exits to get drinks)

SOPHIA   Seeing quite a bit of Mr. Wallbanger tonight.

MARTHA   I'm celebrating because I've just had an idea that will change my life. Order anything you like. I'm going to have the shrimp cocktail, the cream of mushroom soup, asparagus with hollandaise sauce and the filet mignon.

SOPHIA   I like cholesterol as much as the next guy, but you're never going to get blood to your feet again.
(Bartender brings drinks)

MARTHA   I'd like to drink a toast.
(They both raise glasses)
To Sophia, whom I hope I can count on.

SOPHIA   For what? Get your lips off Harvey and tell me what you want.

MARTHA   Since you mentioned it, I want you to do something for me. I want you to come over to my place tomorrow night.

SOPHIA   Oh, what is it, your birthday?

MARTHA   Sophia, there aren't going to be any more birthdays.

SOPHIA   What're you telling me?

MARTHA   *(Sighs)* I have so many things wrong with me – arthritis, high blood pressure, angina, just to mention a few.

SOPHIA   Who doesn't? You can't get into our canasta game unless you have at least two debilitating diseases.
(Maitre D' approaches)

MAITRE D'   Your table is ready, madams.
(Sophia lifts arms up to be taken down from chair. Maitre D' lifts her down)

SOPHIA	I don't know. For me it was better the first time. What do you think?
MAITRE D'	Right this way, please.
SOPHIA	So, why do you want me to be at your house tomorrow?
MARTHA	I want you to be there when I kill myself.

ACT ONE

Scene 4

KITCHEN – NIGHT

(Dorothy holds screaming baby. Blanche tries to read thermometer. Rose at stove)

DOROTHY	What is it, Blanche?
BLANCHE	Oh, I can't quite make it out. I think my eyes are tired.
DOROTHY	Your eyes are old. Blanche, when are you gonna admit you need glasses?
BLANCHE	I do not need glasses. My mother didn't need glasses 'til the day she died. And then it seemed silly.
DOROTHY	What is his temperature, Blanche?
BLANCHE	*(Holds out thermometer)* I do not know, Dorothy. Even with perfect eyesight, nobody can read one of these things.
ROSE	My God, it's a hundred are three point two.
DOROTHY	The poor baby.
ROSE	Oh, we better contact his parents.
DOROTHY	They're out in the woods somewhere. W-We better call Harry. We're very lucky we have a pediatrician right down the street.

BLANCHE   No, that's a bad idea.

DOROTHY   Why?

BLANCHE   Because by the time I get my hair done and my face on, that baby could be in serious trouble. Let's call his real pediatrician.
(Rose looks at baby instructions of fridge door)

ROSE   Okay, pediatrician. Pedia – here it is – Doctor Harry Weston!
(Dorothy dials phone)

BLANCHE   Oh God.

DOROTHY   Oh come on, Blanche, he's a doctor. Used to seeing people at their worst. And if you comb your hair, you can be right in that ballpark.
(Into phone)
Harry? Y-Dorothy. Uh, Yeah, listen, I'm y-so sorry I have to call you at home. But, we're taking care of the Lillestrand baby and he'd running a very high fever. Yeah, could you come over right away. No, this is not Blanche playing a joke. Thanks, Harry. Thanks very much.
(She hangs up phone)

BLANCHE   He's coming?

DOROTHY   Right away.

BLANCHE   Oh, dear, I better freshen up.

DOROTHY   Blanche, he is not coming over to look at you. He's coming over to look at the baby.

BLANCHE   I'll be holding the baby next to my bosom. What a magnificent picture. God, I wish that thing didn't look so sickly.
(Blanche exits)

ACT ONE
Scene 5

LE MARMITON RESTAURANT – NIGHT (SIMULTANEOUS)
(Sophia and Martha at table)

SOPHIA I don't care if you are paying for dinner. What you want to do is crazy.

MARTHA It's time to go, Sophia. I don't want to see another Monday. I don't want to wait and end up going like Lydia. *I'm* going to decide when it's over.

SOPHIA I always thought somebody named God did that.

MARTHA You don't understand. I'm afraid of the pain, of the hurting. I'm afraid of being alone. Of dying alone. I can take the pills myself. But I want you to be there and hold my hand.

SOPHIA You're right. I don't understand. I'd do anything to stay alive. If my heart stopped beating, I'd want every doctor in town jumping up and down on my chest.

MARTHA You say that now, but I don't have the courage to die by inches. I'm going to do it whether you're there or not. I don't want to die alone. Please help me.

END OF ACT ONE

ACT TWO
Scene 1

LIVING ROOM – A LITTLE LATER THAT NIGHT
(Dorothy holds crying baby. Rose changes carriage sheet. Blanche enters in negligee, putting on earrings)

BLANCHE	Dorothy, do you think this looks alluring and yet nurse-like?
DOROTHY	I don't know, Blanche, maybe the earrings put it over the top.
BLANCHE	No, I did that for the baby. They love shiny things . . . Listen, maybe you two ought to wait in the kitchen with the kid. DOORBELL
ROSE	Oh, I'll get it.
BLANCHE	Freeze! Don't go near that door. Give me that thing. *(Blanche grabs baby from Dorothy, goes to door and poses with it)* *(To baby)* Hello, Frank, darling. Nnnh. *(To ladies)* How do I look?
DOROTHY	It's all wrong, Blanche. The baby doesn't match your shoes. *(Blanche opens door. Harry enters)*
HARRY	Hello, ladies. Hi there, how are you?
DOROTHY	Oh, Harry, thanks so much for coming over.
HARRY	*(To baby in Blanche's arms)* Frank, Frank, talk to me. What's going on here?
BLANCHE	Well, he isn't feeling very well, so we thought we'd have you over for a drink.
DOROTHY	Hey, why don't we just forget the baby and go dancing?
HARRY	Blanche, that is some outfit. *(Blanche giggles seductively)* What do you call that?
BLANCHE	A negligee.

HARRY	Brings back fond memories.
BLANCHE	Hhmmm . . .
HARRY	My mother used to have one just like it. *(Blanche hands baby to Dorothy, crushed)*
BLANCHE	Here, take him. He's wet.
HARRY	Well, somebody'd better change him or he'll get a rash on his winkie.
DOROTHY	We're sorry we had to disturb you, Harry, but he's running a fever of a hundred and three.
BLANCHE	What do you think it is?
HARRY	Well, he could be teething, it could be the flu, and maybe he's just a hypochondriac.
ROSE	Really?
HARRY	Well, let's take a look. *(To baby)* So you've been keeping these ladies busy, have you? *(He starts examining baby)*
BLANCHE	Oh, I didn't mind. I have such a highly-developed maternal instinct.
HARRY	I, I-I-I was talking to the baby, Blanche. A-A-Any other symptoms, rash, uh . . .
ROSE	No. He was fine one minute and running a fever the next.
HARRY	*(To baby)* Is it the usual? Huh? *(To ladies)* Yeah, Frank tends to get ear infections from time to time.
DOROTHY	Is he gonna be all right?
HARRY	Oh, he'll be fine. He'll be fine. We'll just keep a close watch on him.

(*Take medicine bottle from bag*)
Give him four drops of this right now, and then once every two hours. Give him plenty of fluids so he doesn't get dehydrated. Hey, and I'll check back on you tomorrow.
(*Harry gives baby to Rose*)

BLANCHE When are we supposed to sleep?
(*Catching herself*)
Not that I mind.
(*Moving in on Harry*)
I was born to heal.

DOROTHY Heel, Blanche.

HARRY Welcome back to motherhood, ladies. I'm sure you were good mothers and you remember what to do. Blanche, watch the others, you look like you pick up things quickly. Gotta go.
(*Harry exits*)

ACT TWO
Scene 2

LIVING ROOM – (*3: 00 AM*)
(*Dorothy and Rose sit on couch watching Blanche push crying baby around in pram*)

BLANCHE What is wrong with this baby? Honey, darlin', please shut up for Aunt Blanche.

ROSE You know, back in St. Olaf we had a surefire method for getting babies to sleep.

DOROTHY If herring, elk or anyone named Sven figures in this, I don't want to hear it.

ROSE Okay, I've got another one. Whenever my kids couldn't sleep, we always sang to them.

BLANCHE A lullaby?

ROSE   Well, sort of. "Mister Sandman."

DOROTHY   Oh, I don't know, Rose.

BLANCHE   Dorothy, come on. It's worth a try. It's either we sing or he sings.

DOROTHY   Oh, all right.

ROSE   *(Singing)* "BOOM . . ."
(Waits a beat for them to join in. They don't)
"BOOM . . ."
(Pause)
Well?

BLANCHE   Well, what?

ROSE   After my "Boom" comes your "Boom" and then yours. Until we're all "Booming."

DOROTHY   How complicated is that herring thing?
(They start tentatively, build until singing full out)

ROSE   ". . . BOOM . . ."

BLANCHE   ". . . BOOM . . ."

BLANCHE/ ". . . BOOM, BOOM, BOOM, BOOM,
DOROTHY BOOM, BOOM . . ."

ROSE   ". . . BOOM . . ."

BLANCHE/ ". . . BOOM, BOOM, BOOM, BOOM . . ."
DOROTHY

ROSE   ". . . BOOM . . ."

BLANCHE/ ". . . BOOM, BOOM, BOOM, BOOM,
DOROTHY BOOM, BOOM, BOOM . . ."

ROSE   ". . . BOOM . . ."

BLANCHE/ ". . . BOOM, BOOM, BOOM, BOOM . . ."
DOROTHY

ROSE/   *(Singing)* "MISTER SANDMAN, BRING ME
DOROTHY/ A DREAM . . ."
BLANCHE

DOROTHY	"... BOOM, BOOM, BOOM, BOOM ..."
ROSE/ DOROTHY/ BLANCHE	"MAKE HIM THE CUTEST THAT I'VE EVER SEEN ..."
DOROTHY	"... BOOM, BOOM, BOOM, BOOM ..."
ROSE/ DOROTHY/ BLANCHE	"GIVE HIM TWO LIPS LIKE ROSES AND CLOVER ..."
DOROTHY	"... BOOM, BOOM, BOOM, BOOM ..."
ROSE/ DOROTHY/ BLANCHE	"THEN TELL HIM THAT HIS LONESOME NIGHTS ARE OVER ..." *(Baby stops crying. The ladies stop singing. They start to sneak away, but baby immediately cries again. They begin singing again)*
ROSE	"BOOM ..."
BLANCHE/ DOROTHY	"... BOOM, BOOM, BOOM, BOOM, BOOM, BOOM, BOOM ..."
ROSE	"... BOOM ..."
BLANCHE/ DOROTHY	"... BOOM, BOOM, BOOM, BOOM ..."
ROSE	"... BOOM ..."
BLANCHE/ DOROTHY	"... BOOM, BOOM, BOOM, BOOM, BOOM, BOOM, BOOM ..."
ROSE	"... BOOM ..."
BLANCHE/ DOROTHY	"... BOOM, BOOM, BOOM, BOOM ..."
ROSE/ DOROTHY/ BLANCHE	"MISTER SANDMAN ..." Yeeessss ... *Again crying stops. During the following Sophia enters from hallway, watches them)* "...BRING ME A DREAM ... MAKE HIM THE CUTEST THAT I'VE

EVER SEEN . . .
GIVE HIM THE WORD THAT I'M NOT A
ROVER . . .
THEN TELL HIM THAT HIS LONESOME
NIGHTS ARE OVER . . .
MISTER SANDMAN, I'M SO ALONE . . .
I'M . . .
(When they stop:)

SOPHIA   Boy, you guys really stink.

DOROTHY   We were just singing the baby to sleep.

SOPHIA   It was waking me up.

BLANCHE   Maybe we oughta go out in the kitchen.

ROSE   So we can talk.

BLANCHE   So we can eat.

ROSE   Better.
(They exit to kitchen)

ACT TWO
Scene 3

KITCHEN – NIGHT (CONTINUOUS)
(The ladies enter)

DOROTHY   Ma, we're sorry our singing woke you.

SOPHIA   It wasn't you. I had a horrible nightmare. I
dreamt my Uncle Giuseppe came down from
heaven and was pointing a finger at me . . .I
think it was a finger . . . and he was warning me
if I did a certain thing I wouldn't get into
heaven.

DOROTHY   What thing?

SOPHIA   Try murder.

ROSE	It was just a dream, Sophia.
SOPHIA	It's not just a dream for me. Martha wants to commit suicide and she wants me to be there with her.
BLANCHE	And what did you say?
SOPHIA	I said I'd think about it. You can't say no to somebody who pops for a seventy-five dollar dinner. Tell them, Blanche.
DOROTHY	Ma, I can't believe that you're seriously considering getting involved in this.
SOPHIA	Martha's a sick woman and she doesn't want to get any sicker. She's going to do it anyway, so why should she die alone?
ROSE	This is wrong, Sophia.
DOROTHY	Forget about whether this is right or wrong. Ma, I'm worried about *you*. When Martha takes those pills or, or whatever and, and the life drains out of her, you're gonna be in that room – alone. What are you gonna do, Ma? How are you gonna feel?
SOPHIA	I don't know, but I'll deal with it.
BLANCHE	When my time comes, I sure want somebody to put me out of my misery if something tragic happens, like I get a fatal illness or I've lost my looks.
DOROTHY	Tell us when, Blanche . . . *(To Sophia)* Ma, I forbid you to do this.
SOPHIA	Dorothy, sometimes you forget, I'm the mother here.
DOROTHY	That has nothing to do with this.
SOPHIA	It has everything to do with this. In the

twenty-five years I have on you, I've learned
something.
(Searching)
I just wish I could remember what it is. Oh,
yeah, I-I got it. It's not whether you agree or
disagree with somebody, it's whether you can
be there for that person when they need you.

ROSE   Sophia, I can't believe you're doing this. You
        know, this reminds me of the story of Gunilla
        Ulfstadder, St. Olaf's very own Angel of Death.

DOROTHY *(Encouraging)* Tell it, Rose, tell it.

ROSE   Really? All the way through?

DOROTHY All the way through. But please try to make the
        end come as close to the beginning as possible.

ROSE   Well, Gunilla Ulfstadder was a nurse at Cedar's
        of St. Olaf Hospital. One night she was taking
        care of Sven Bjornson, and he asked her if she
        would get him some more mouth moisteners
        and then kill him. Gunilla brought the mouth
        moisteners right way, but the killing thing –
        uh, it seemed to go against everything she'd
        been taught.

DOROTHY Y-You're doing beautifully, Rose.

ROSE   Well, he begged and he begged, and by her
        coffee break she couldn't stand it anymore. So
        she pulled the plug, and he died. Well, she was
        wracked with guilt that night. Not only had she
        parked her car in a doctor's spot, but she was
        never sure whether Sven's pleading was the
        pain talking, or the medication talking, or the
        guy in the next bed talking You see, the guy in
        the next bed was Ingmar von Burgen, St. Olaf's
        meanest ventriloquist.

DOROTHY Rose, we are going somewhere with this, aren't

	we? I mean, if not, I'm gonna cut out your tongue.
ROSE	Yes, Sven came back to haunt Gunilla. Since then, every Tuesday night at ten, nine Central –
DOROTHY	*(Bangs table, fed up)* Oh . . .!
ROSE	– she hears noises. Some say it's the wind. But some say it's Sven's voice whispering back from the other side, saying, "Turn around quick, his lips are moving."
DOROTHY	You see that, Ma? You kill someone, you end up being a Rose story. Is this what you want?
SOPHIA	Dorothy, I'll worry about me later. I gotta do this. Good night, pussycat. *(Sophia exits)*

ACT TWO
Scene 4

MARTHA'S APARTMENT – NEXT NIGHT
(Martha is just answering the door. It's Sophia)

MARTHA	You came.
SOPHIA	*(Entering)* I said I would.
MARTHA	Come in. Come in and sit down. I have something to show you. *(They sit on sofa. Martha shows off diamond ring)* Look, ten carats and not a flaw . . . I bought it today . . . on time, ha ha.
SOPHIA	Very nice. Look, I was thinking, maybe you shouldn't go through with this right . . .
MARTHA	*(Overlapping her)* No, I have to go. I've never

felt so happy . . . Do you like the ring?

SOPHIA   Reminds me of a doorknob I had back in
         Brooklyn.
         Martha laughs, give ring to Sophia)
         What are you doing?

MARTHA   Just my way of saying thank you. Well, I think
         I've taken care of everything. Now you'll see to
         it that they don't put lipstick on my teeth?

SOPHIA   Don't worry. I'll take them out and check them
         personally.
         (Martha crosses off list)

MARTHA   Well, I guess, uh, it's time to go.
         Takes bottle of pills from table)
         You will hold my hand?

SOPHIA   Sure I will.

MARTHA   I'm so glad I don't have to go alone.
         (Martha uncaps bottle)

SOPHIA   Uh, you remember how we met?

MARTHA   Yes, about eight years ago? We shared a room
         in the hospital. You had the heart scare. I was
         the gall bladder.

SOPHIA   They gave you my sponge bath by mistake.

MARTHA   You ate my jello. It was a horrible little room.
         We couldn't wait to get out of it.

SOPHIA   Because we wanted to live.

MARTA   Yes, I remember.

SOPHIA   Remember better. Remember life.

MARTHA · I don't have much of one. I'm not like you. You
         live with friends and family . . .holidays and
         warmth. I hear the silence.

SOPHIA   We'll talk. We'll talk all the time. You can
         come over Thanksgiving, Christmas, every

Friday night. I may not be there, but you can always talk to Rose.

MARTHA   No, I want to go. Lydia looked so peaceful. *(Sophia takes bottle of pills)*

SOPHIA   We're not in this life for peace.

MARTHA   You're crying.

SOPHIA   No, I'm not. I don't cry.

MARTHA   I can see your tears.

SOPHIA   And I can see yours. You know what that tells me?

MARTHA   What?

SOPHIA   You're not as ready to die as you think you are. You still want to live, kid.

MARTHA   Some kid. I don't know what to do.

SOPHIA   That's the point. If you're not sure, you can't change your mind tomorrow. You wanted me to be here for your death. How about letting me be here for your life?

MARTHA   Like a friend?

SOPHIA   Like a best friend. *(The two women embrace)*

ACT TWO
Scene 5

KITCHEN – AN HOUR LATER
(Blanche holds baby. Rose has thermometer under baby's arms. Dorothy paces)

BLANCHE   Dorothy, honey, sit down. Pacing isn't gonna help.

DOROTHY   I just can't stop thinking about Ma.

ROSE	*(Removes thermometer)* Look at that. Perfect, Ninety-eight point six.
BLANCHE	Yep, that's what it looks like to me.
DOROTHY	Thank God, that means he's better.
BLANCHE	Here, I'm pooped. *(She hands baby to Rose)* Oh, I guess there must be a reason why women have babies when they're twentyish instead of fortyish.
DOROTHY	Blanche, the only thing in this room that's fortyish is your hairdo. *(Sophia enters)* Ma.
SOPHIA	It's okay. She changed her mind.
DOROTHY	Oh, Ma, thank God . . .
BLANCHE	*(Simultaneous with Dorothy)* Oh.
SOPHIA	I know, Dorothy. I know. *DOORBELL*
ROSE	Oh, that must be the Lillestrands.
DOROTHY	Frank, we love you but you are out of here. *(Rose and Blanche exit)*
SOPHIA	*(To Dorothy)* Give me a minute.
DOROTHY	Sure. *(Dorothy exits)*
SOPHIA	*(Lifts baby)* Listen, you, you're just starting out. You're in for the long haul. Keep your seatbelt on, there are lots of twists and turns. *(Gives baby hug. Baby starts to cry)* Stop that, or they're going to come in here and sing again. *(Crying stops)* END OF ACT TWO

COMEDY
of
ERRORS

Written by: DON REO
Directed by: TERRY HUGHES

· *Introduction* ·

THE RECURRENT PROBLEM of insecurity threads its way through every page of this episode. Normally featured on screens both big and small as the exclusive province of beleagered parents, handwringing divorcees or tortured teens, it presents itself here as a day-to-day hazard of later middle-age.

Dorothy, normally the warm, steady voice of reassurance, is beset with a rare attack of brooding self-analysis after running into an old school chum, Helen Colquist:

"She just moved to Miami. And we spent a little time together and decided we'd get together today. I even got out the old yearbook so we could go down memory lane. Last night she had a heart attack and died."

Yet, even as Dorothy reels off her former classmates who are now dead (several heart attacks and a high-speed car crash), the scene is continually punctured with Sophia's rapier wit:

"That's my pussycat, fun, fun, fun."

As uncertainty invades her every thought, Dorothy pleads openly that she is only "a substitute teacher. I'll never be rich before I'm twenty-one. I'll never be homecoming queen." She finally admits that her own American Dream has always been to stand on a stage and crack jokes, despite Sophia's insistence that Dorothy "went to a special school for the dull."

After much supportive prodding from her friends, and a plethora of unhelpful but amusing asides from her mother, Dorothy takes the stage during amateur night at a local comedy club. After a few apologies and defensive remarks, Dorothy suddenly erupts into a stream-of-consciousness spiel in which she verbally knocks out her mother ("the incredible shrinking woman") before outlining her domestic life with her friends:

"You know, at our ages, the four of us being together, the same house, we go through so many hormone changes that, uh, some nights we can actually read by the hot flashes."

Rose, meanwhile, has also been swamped by insecurity because she cannot deal with not being liked. Having discovered that being nice led to instant popularity ("Dorothy, you're the smart one, and Blanche, you're the sexy one and Sophia, you're the old one and I'm the nice one"), she now reacts badly to the hostility shown her by Roger, a colleague at the office.

The serious roots of her anxiety are laid bare ("you see only the happy, nice kids got adopted and that's when I started trying to be happy and nice all the time"), while the episode ends on a familiar comic note as Rose tries to befriend Roger through baking him a cake and buying him a cat.

In this episode, the normally sassy Blanche also has the rug of certainty yanked from under her. Having received a sharp letter from the Inland Revenue or, as she more bluntly puts it, "filth through the mail", Blanche displays fecklessness, vulnerability and a keen desire to attract the taxman in order to lighten the many moments of intensity.

CAST

DOROTHY, ROSE, BLANCHE, SOPHIA, ROGER BARTON, RONNY LARK, GLORIA SCHMIDT, COMIC.

ACT ONE
Scene 1

LIVING ROOM – DAY
(Dorothy on couch. Blanche enters front with mail. Hands Dorothy mail)

DOROTHY   Thank you.
            (Blanche opens an envelope, gets mad)

BLANCHE   Oh. Oh, a person cannot open a letter anymore without being accosted by some vile, disgusting thing. I thought it was against the law to send filth like this through the mail!

DOROTHY   Oh, no, what is it, Blanche?

BLANCHE   A letter from the IRS. I am being audited!

DOROTHY   Oh, it's aggravating, yes, but you don't have anything to be worried about.
            (Blanche looks guilty)
            Do you?

BLANCHE   Well, of course not. But you know how nitpicky they can be. You forget to dot one little "i" or you don't declare the tiniest little thing, and they can blow it all out of proportion.

DOROTHY   What didn't you declare, Blanche?

BLANCHE   You.

DOROTHY   Me?

BLANCHE   And Rose and Sophia. I think over the past five years I might have forgotten to mention that

	y'all are living here with me and paying rent.
DOROTHY	We just slipped your mind?
BLANCHE	Well, of course not, darlin'. But you know I think of you girls as family. Now how would it look if they thought I was charging my own family rent?
DOROTHY	Honest.
BLANCHE	Don't you ever get a nosebleed from taking the high road all the time? Oh, this is such an upsetting day.
DOROTHY	For both of us.
BLANCHE	Why, what's wrong with you?
DOROTHY	Oh, I ran into an old friend of mine from high school. Helen Colquist. She just moved to Miami. And we spent a little time together and decided we'd get together today. I even got out the old yearbook so we could go down memory lane.
BLANCHE	Oh.
DOROTHY	Last night she had a heart attack and died.
BLANCHE	Oh, I'm sorry.
DOROTHY	Yeah, I've been sitting here looking through the book, and I can't believe how many of my classmates are gone.
BLANCHE	Hmmm . . .
DOROTHY	*(Looks at book)* I mean, look. Frank Bonitardi. Tight end on the football team. Heart attack. Dead.
BLANCHE	Well, Dorothy, don't think of it as Frank being dead. Just think of it as God telling Frank to go deep.
DOROTHY	*(Back to book)*

Oh . . . David Brittingham . . .

BLANCHE   What happened to him?

DOROTHY   God told David to drive into a wall at eighty miles an hour.
(*Sophia enters*)

SOPHIA   What are you doing?

BLANCHE   Dorothy's going through her high school yearbook to see who all's dead.

SOPHIA   That's my pussycat, fun, fun, fun.

DOROTHY   Ma, do you remember Helen Colquist?

SOPHIA   Was she that tremendously fat woman with a wooden leg and a totally hairless cat named Cincinnati Jake?

DOROTHY   No.

SOPHIA   Then I don't remember her.

DOROTHY   Oh, Ma, look at this. A list I made of things I wanted to do with my life . . .

BLANCHE   You know, I had a list like that, and I've done most of them . . . except for Burt Lancaster.

DOROTHY   I haven't done half the things on this list. I mean, what am I? I am a substitute teacher. I'll never be rich before I'm twenty-one. I'll never be homecoming queen . . .

SOPHIA   You can still be homecoming queen. It'll just be a different kind of home.

BLANCHE   What else is on your list, Dorothy?

DOROTHY   Uh, I wanted to entertain people.

BLANCHE   (*Laughs, greatly amused*)
You? An entertainer?

DOROTHY   Well, yes. I was in the drama club. I was also voted the most humourous girl in my class.

SOPHIA	She went to a special school for the dull.
DOROTHY	I did not.
SOPHIA	Okay, it's time for dinner.
BLANCHE	Dorothy, tell me something else that's on your list. An entertainer . . . (*She laughs again as they exit to kitchen*)

ACT ONE
Scene 2

KITCHEN – DAY (CONTINUOUS)

DOROTHY	Entertaining people, getting my masters and I wanted to sleep with Michael Delvecchio.
BLANCHE	Wait a minute. Michael Delvecchio? Is he tall, with black hair, has a mole on his cheek? Sells insurance in New York City?
DOROTHY	Yes!
BLANCHE	You didn't miss much.
DOROTHY	The point is, I didn't do any of the things on my list. I mean, all my dreams went unfulfilled. You know, the other day I was talking to Helen Colquist – she said she always wanted to go to the Holy Land. She had just bought the ticket. Now she's dead. (*Rose enters*)
ROSE	Hi. What a day.
DOROTHY	Oh, you, too?
ROSE	Oh . . . you know Roger Barton, the man who works in the cubicle next to me? He doesn't like me. Everybody's always liked me.
BLANCHE	Honey, maybe your chemistry's just off. Everybody doesn't have to like you.

ROSE   Oh, yes, they do. Dorothy, you're the smart one, and Blanche, you're the sexy one, and Sophia, you're the old one and I'm the nice one. Everybody always likes me.

SOPHIA   The old one isn't so crazy about you.

ROSE   Roger likes everybody else in the office. I don't know why he doesn't like me. I go out of my way to be friendly. You know that happy thought of the day that I write down and give to everyone? He doesn't even like that. But I have a plan.

BLANCHE   What is your plan?

ROSE   His dog died.

DOROTHY   That's your plan?

ROSE   No, I'm gonna replace his dog.

DOROTHY   Rose, you don't even like bringing me *my* slippers.

ROSE   No, I'm gonna get him a new pet to replace his. His dog lifted his leg on an electric fence. Poor Sparky. To show him how sorry I am, I'm gonna go to the pound and get him another pet.

BLANCHE   Uh, Rose, I really think you're trying a little too hard.

DOROTHY   Oh, I don't. I don't. No, Rose, I admire you. When you want something to happen, you go for it. Me? I dream.

SOPHIA   Are you back on that showbiz kick again?

DOROTHY   Oh, yeah, Ma. You know, I was always pretty good at it – even way back in high school. Ma, do you remember those variety shows that my class used to put on? I was really very good. You know, I'd get up there and tell a few jokes about

the teachers, about the cafeteria food. Ma, do you remember, ". . . you call this tapioca?"
(Dorothy laughs)

SOPHIA   Timeless.

DOROTHY   The kids really liked me. I mean, they laughed. I felt great.

BLANCHE   Oh, Dorothy, if there's something you're aching to do, then you simply have to do it. Do you remember when we went to amateur night at the Comedy Barrel? Honey, I know you've got to be as good as some of those people.

DOROTHY   I couldn't. I'm . . . I'd be up there sweating bullets.

SOPHIA   And dodging some.

ROSE   No, you should try it, Dorothy. And we'd be right there, front and centre, cheering you on.

DOROTHY   Oh, no, this is crazy. I mean, what if I die out there?

SOPHIA   Ah, who cares if you stink? Who cares if nobody laughs? Who cares if you make a fool of yourself?

DOROTHY   I care.

SOPHIA   Then you got problems.

ACT ONE
Scene 3

LIVING ROOM – NEXT DAY

(Rose is alone)

DOORBELL

ROSE   Coming.
(She opens door. It's Roger Barton. In one hand he

carries a cat cage. Other hand is not in view)
Roger! Oh, Roger, I can't tell you how sorry I am about what happened to Sparky. And how are you?

ROGER   I've been better, Rose. I've come to talk to you about this cat you sent me.

ROSE   When I saw him at the pound I knew he'd be just the cat for you. I named him "Buster". Isn't he precious?

ROGER   *(Revealing bandaged hand)*
He mauled me, Rose.

ROSE   Buster did that? But he seemed so sweet.

ROGER   Well, he may be, Rose, but he just doesn't like me. Sometimes in life that happens. For instance, I don't like you.

ROSE   But everybody likes me.

ROGER   Can't say that anymore, Rose.

ROSE   Do you really hate me?

ROGER   Oh yeah. Now, ah, here's Buster back.
(Hands cat cage to Rose)

ROSE   Well, you told me you were an animal lover, and I thought maybe I could replace your loss.

ROGER   Well, I didn't need a replacement. You see, I had my parakeet. Or, I used to have him until you sent that cat from hell into our lives.

ROSE   You don't mean . . .

ROGER   Yeah, I don't think you're gonna have to feed Buster for a while. Goodbye, Rose, and when you see me at work, don't say good morning. Don't leave me those cheery notes. And please don't put on those little puppet shows over the partition. In fact, don't ever think of me again.
(He exits. Sophia enters, peeks into cat cage)

SOPHIA	Oh, whose cat is this?
ROSE	Well actually, I got it at the pound for somebody and now they don't want him.
SOPHIA	I was talking to Sara Antonelli the other day. She's got a cellar full of mice and she needs a cat. You think this guy's got the killer instinct?
ROSE	Oh, I think so. Please take him, Sophia. His name is Buster. *(Sophia begins to exit with cat)*
SOPHIA	He sure is cute. I love the way he's got that jaunty little yellow feather behind his ear. *(Sophia makes kissy noises at the cat)* Kitty, kitty, kitty! *(Sophia exits)*

ACT ONE
Scene 4

KITCHEN – THAT NIGHT
(Dorothy at table, writing jokes. Blanche enters with shoe box)

DOROTHY	What's in the shoe box, Blanche?
BLANCHE	Every last receipt and scrap of paper I have collected over the last five years. *(Opens shoe box)* Or a pair of shoes. *(Takes out shoes)* Dorothy, what am I gonna do? I'm meeting with my accountant tomorrow. He said to bring everything.
DOROTHY	Then you better include a cake with a file in it. Where are your receipts, Blanche?
BLANCHE	I always thought you only needed a receipt if the dress you bought didn't fit. I'm just no good at this.

DOROTHY	Yeah, that's beginning to shine through.
BLANCHE	It was so much easier when I was married. I'd buy something expensive, George would yell at me, I'd put on a see-through nightie and that'd be the end of it. Why can't the government work that way?
DOROTHY	According to the newspapers, a lot of times it does. Uh, this money that you forgot to give to the IRS – what did you do with it?
BLANCHE	Well, I can't remember what I did with every penny. I know I gave some of it to charity.
DOROTHY	Charitable deductions, Blanche, that's great. What was it – United Fund, Greenpeace, you remember?
BLANCHE	In 1985 I bought the "We Are The World" album. *(Blanche exits, as Sophia enters)*
SOPHIA	Dorothy, have you seen my teeth?
DOROTHY	They're in your mouth, Ma.
SOPHIA	I know that. Don't they look good today? I ran them through the dishwasher.
DOROTHY	Ma, listen to me, you got Martha Raye and Madge mixed up again.
SOPHIA	Oh yeah.
DOROTHY	Listen, Ma, would you like to listen to a joke?
SOPHIA	Is this from your act?
DOROTHY	Eh, could be. I, uh, went down to the Comedy Barrel and signed up for Monday night. Lemme try this out on you.
SOPHIA	Okay. Make me laugh.
DOROTHY	All right, here we go. It seems there was this doctor –

SOPHIA	"It seems" there was? What is this, existentialist humour? Was there a doctor or wasn't there?
DOROTHY	Yes. Yes, there was this doctor. He's sitting in the park –
SOPHIA	What time of year is it?
DOROTHY	What difference does it make?
SOPHIA	You have to set the scene.
DOROTHY	Who is telling this joke?
SOPHIA	At the moment nobody.
DOROTHY	You know, Ma, it would be very nice if you could be a little supportive.
SOPHIA	Please, I've always been supportive. Remember when you wanted to run away to Canada so you wouldn't get drafted?
DOROTHY	Ma, that was my brother Phil.
SOPHIA	Oh, yeah. I get confused. He was wearing your dress. Okay, how about when you were unmarried and pregnant?
DOROTHY	Ah! I remember your exact words: "Get out of my house. You're dead. I have no daughter named Dorothy."
SOPHIA	Sure, in that tone of voice it sounds bad. But I'm supporting you now. Didn't I come here to live with you in your twilight years?
DOROTHY	Ma, these are your twilight years.
SOPHIA	Are you kidding? I'm supposed to be dead. These are *your* twilight years!
DOROTHY	Ma, I never needed you more. I'm about to do something that is very important to me. I mean, I could fall flat on my face.
SOPHIA	Fall the other way, it's funnier.

END OF ACT ONE

ACT TWO
Scene 1

LIVING ROOM – NEXT DAY
(Dorothy and Sophia are there. Sophia has stopwatch and is timing Dorothy's act)

DOROTHY . . . Thank you, and good night.
(Sophia stops watch)
Well, Ma?

SOPHIA Five mintues and ten seconds.

DOROTHY Ah, that's a little long. What should I cut?

SOPHIA After hearing that act, your throat.
(Blanche enters)

DOROTHY Oh, hi, Blanche. How did it go at the accountant's?

BLANCHE Oh, just fine. Hey, while I was in the waiting room, I was reading a magazine that listed the ten richest men in America. Y'know, Merv Griffin's moved up a couple of notches.

DOROTHY He probably ate the two guys ahead of him.

BLANCHE Anyway, I got good news from my accountant. I'm being audited Tuesday.

DOROTHY Oh, lucky you.

BLANCHE Oh, but Dorothy, you don't get it. My accountant reminded me that I've been audited before and I've never had to pay a penny in back taxes. I have a way with auditors. The last time I was audited I got money back from the government.

SOPHIA Blanche, it's not a refund when the auditor leaves two twenties on your nightstand.
(Rose enters from kitchen with cake box)

ROSE Do you want to see my vanskap kaka?

SOPHIA	As long as I don't have to show you mine.
ROSE	It's a St. Olaf friendship cake. I'm taking it to Roger. It's made with milk, sugar, honey, a whole lot of love and just a drop of sunshine.
BLANCHE	Honey, why don't you leave the poor man alone?
ROSE	I know if he got to know me, he'd like me.
SOPHIA	Why? I got to know you. I don't like you.
ROSE	You just say that.
SOPHIA	Repeatedly. *(Rose laughs)*
DOROTHY	Rose, you've become obsessed. You have this irrational need to get Roger to like you. Now, why are you doing this?
ROSE	I guess it all started when I was a little kid at the orphanage. You see, only the happy, nice kids got adopted and that's when I started trying to be happy and nice all the time. 'Cause the truth is, if you treat somebody really nicely, they'll take you home.
BLANCHE	I've always found that to be true.
ROSE	*(Sighs)* Right now I feel like the little kid at the orphanage.
BLANCHE	Okay, Rose. I'm gonna tell you a little story about a young girl in high school who was very insecure about the other kids liking her. Now she would do anything, anything to gain their approval. She would do their homework for them while her grades suffered. She would give them her lunch money in the misguided belief that she could buy their acceptance. Finally, lonely and desperate for affection, she gave her virginity to the first boy who showed her the slightest attention.

DOROTHY   Oh. You know, Blanche, until you told this
           story, I-I never realized how much we had in
           common.

BLANCHE   We don't have anything in common. That was
           a story Sophia told me about you.

DOROTHY   Rose, the point is, there's always gonna be
           somebody who doesn't like you.

ROSE   Yes, and when you find that one person, you
           have to try even harder to get them to like you.
           Did I ever tell you the story about Herde
           Shornbohrst?

BLANCHE   Many, many times.

DOROTHY   Yes, yes, yes.

SOPHIA   Yes, you have.

ROSE   Well, then you remember he was St. Olaf's
           most famous shepherd. Well, Herde used to
           say, you can have a hundred sheep and if one
           goes astray, that's the one you go look for.
           Especially if it's the best-looking one.
           (Rose exits)

DOROTHY   Rose has got to find some new role models.

ACT TWO
Scene 2

APARTMENT HALLWAY – DAY
(Rose enters from elevator, approaches Roger's door with care
box. She rings doorbell)

DOORBELL
(Roger opens door)

ROGER   Rose. I was just thinking about you.

ROSE   Really?

ROGER	Yeah. My hand was throbbing.
ROSE	I brought you a vanskap kaka. It's a traditional St. Olaf friendship cake.
ROGER	Rose, I don't want any gifts from you. I mean, I really don't want to have anything to do with you. Let me ask you something. Uh, uh, what is your idea of a friend?
ROSE	Well, a friend is someone who likes you and, respects you and, is willing to do things for you.
ROGER	So, if, uh, I was your friend, you'd be willing to do things for me and respect my wishes?
ROSE	Of course. I'd have to.
ROGER	Well, I've asked you to leave me alone and you haven't. I mean, what kind of friend is that?
ROSE	Well, you said you weren't my friend.
ROGER	Well, what if I say I am your friend?
ROSE	Well, then I'd have to do it. You'd be my friend.
ROGER	Then we're friends!
ROSE	You mean it?
ROGER	Forever! Ah, just don't forget to leave me alone.
ROSE	Well, that's what friends are for. *(Roger presses button on elevator)*
ROGER	See ya, pal.
ROSE	Thank you, Roger. You don't know what it means to me to hear you say that. *(Roger exits to his apartment, slamming door behind him)* See ya, buddy! *(Rose exits into elevator)*

ACT TWO
Scene 3

BACKSTAGE COMEDY CLUB – NEXT NIGHT
(Dorothy, Blanche, Rose and Sophia are there. Out on stage a comedian is doing his routine)

BLANCHE   You're lookin' awfully pale. Are you all right?

DOROTHY   I was just thinking, how important is it to fulfill your life's dreams? I mean, what's the big deal?

BLANCHE   Now c'mon, Dorothy. You've come this far, you might as well go through with it.

DOROTHY   Yeah, but what if nobody laughs?

SOPHIA   Then you'll know how Lisa Bonet feels.
(Ronny Lark, dressed as M.C., enters and approaches the ladies)

RONNY   Okay, okay, who's got number fourteen?

DOROTHY   *(Whimpering)*
Oh God, I do.

RONNY   Okay, sweetie, you're on next.
(He exits to stage)

ACT TWO
Scene 4

COMEDY CLUB – NIGHT (CONTINUOUS)
(A comic is finishing his act. Audience is laughing. During this, we see Rose, Sophia and Blanche sitting at side table)

COMIC   . . . So, the guy say, "My Saint Bernard, I thought it was *your* Saint Bernard." Ah, I gonna go wash my mouth out with soap. Ah, good night, everybody.
(Comic exits stage to applause)

RONNY   All right, there he goes, the bad boy of comedy, Dirty Dickie Hertz. Not exactly the kind of guy you'd want to meet your mother. Right now, ladies and gentlemen, I want to bring out a lady who actually claims to know which one is Sigfried and which one is Roy, Dorothy "Show Us Your" Zbornak!
(Dorothy steps on stage. Light applause)

DOROTHY   *(Clears throat)* You'll, uh, have to, uh, excuse me. I'm a little nervous. I'm not really a comedian. Whew! Boy, it's a little hot up here.

SOPHIA   How hot is it?

DOROTHY   I-I don't know . . . But it's really hot.

SOPHIA   *(A La Ed McMahon)*
Hi-yo!

DOROTHY   As I said before, my name is Dorothy Zbornak. And, Uh, that's spelled just the way it sounds.

SOPHIA   You're dying. Ask us where we're from.

DOROTHY   That's my mother. The incredible shrinking woman. She's sitting there with the two other women that I live with. You know, at our ages, the four of us living together in the same house, we go through so many hormone changes that, uh, some nights we can actually read by the hot flashes. You know, it's really interesting, when one of us dates an eligible man. Or, as we call them, a live one. Although, it's not really a prerequisite, because I have been known to date a guy on life support. But, uh, the trouble with dating a guy on life support is that you always have to go to his place. Every guy has an angle, you know?

ACT TWO
Scene 5

COMEDY CLUB – FIVE MINUTES LATER
(Dorothy, still on stage, gets big laughs)

DOROTHY   . . .And that's the trouble with the guys here in
Miami. They simply cannot say those three
little words – *(Gasping)*
– "Quick, call 9–1–1!"
(Normally again)
So that's who I am. A substitute teacher with
hot flashes who still lives with her mother, who
heckles her. And I want to thank you for
finding my life more amusing than I do. Good
night. Thank you. You're beautiful. Thank
you.
(They applaud)

ACT TWO
Scene 6

LIVING ROOM – NEXT DAY
(Dorothy is there, Sophia enters from hallway)

SOPHIA   Pussycat, I've been working on some jokes for
your act: "Why did Rose throw the alarm clock
out of the window?"

DOROTHY   I don't know, Ma, why?

SOPHIA   "Because she's a moron."
(Laughs)
I got a million of 'em!

DOROTHY   That's okay, Ma, I don't think I'm gonna be
doing my stand-up routine anymore.

SOPHIA   How come? You were great.

DOROTHY   This morning I realized that what I've been doing is no different from my dream. I mean, every time I stand in front of a classroom, I face the same challenges. Only I come away with something that I didn't feel last night. That maybe, possibly, I've managed to teach them a little something. No, doing stand-up was like having sex with Stan; I was nervous before, it felt pretty good during it, and I'm absolutely *thrilled* that I will never have to do it again.
(Blanche enters in sexy outfit)

BLANCHE   How do I look?

DOROTHY   Oh, is today your audit?

BLANCHE   Yes. He should be here any minute.

DOROTHY   Blanche, how are you going to explain that outfit?

BLANCHE   The zipper's in the back?
DOORBELL
Wish me luck.
(Arranges herself, gets door. Enter Gloria Schmidt)

GLORIA   Blanche Devereaux?

BLANCHE   Yes?

GLORIA   Gloria Schmidt, IRS.

BLANCHE   C'mon in the kitchen, I'll write you a check.
(They exit to kitchen)
END OF ACT TWO

HAVE
YOURSELF
A VERY
LITTLE
CHRISTMAS

Written by: TOM WHEPON
Directed by: TERRY HUGHES

· *Introduction* ·

A TRADITIONALLY SCORCHING Christmas in Miami (Dorothy: "it must be at least a hundred and three") draws out the best side of the four friends which means that even Sophia puts her acid one-liners in storage for the season.

However, instead of turning Christmas festivities into all-out schmaltz, the writers bring in the tough reality of the outside world. While Rose simpers her way through a half-hour rendition of Jingle Bells, Dorothy has been trying to secure a Batman hat for her grandson Robbie:

"I went to six different stores, they were all sold out. I finally went to one store where they had one hat left, and another woman saw it. Oh, I cannot believe a person would push a perfect stranger out of the way, step on her hand and give her an elbow to the forehead just for a Batman hat."

While a comic routine ensues about Christmas gifts of old (young Dorothy's Seven Dwarfs soap soon looked like seven suppositories), the warmly decorated house is cooled a little by the visit of Dorothy's ex-husband Stan, who offers his ex-wife a baseball radio as a present. It came free, naturally, with his subscription to Sports Illustrated. Christmas lights and seasonal bonhomie are swept aside as ten-cents Stan tries to chisel some cash from the foursome.

Stan: "I am planning on opening a research and development lab. We can come up with new and exciting novelties that will make today's plastic vomit obsolete. To make all this happen, all I need from each of you is a thousand dollars. What do you say?"

Relief is written into the proceedings when the girls decide on a system of buying presents by placing names in a hat, while a reassuring comic glow is provided by reminiscences about Christmases past.

Sophia: "And the Mass was in Latin, a fine, old Italian language. Now, who knows? Sometimes it's in English, sometimes in Spanish. If you ask me, they should go back to Latin, the language Jesus spoke."

Dorothy: "Ma, he spoke Hebrew."

Sophia: "Even in church?"

However, the prosaic world beyond the seasonal japes is never far off. Rose, having decided to go to church and serve dinner to Miami's hungry, succeeds in roping in the others. Dorothy shows her usual compassion, Blanche stops thinking about sex and Sophia leaves her deadpan cynicism in the cupboard.

The dramatic function of the Reverend Avery is to describe the situation of America's poor (rents go up, wages are held down, three million homeless in all), while Stan arrives at the church hall as Santa Claus to both create laughter and show that the seasonal spirit can beneficially affect even a rogue hustler.

CAST

<small>DOROTHY, ROSE, BLANCHE, SOPHIA, STAN, REVEREND
AVERY, 3 CAROLERS.</small>

ACT ONE
Scene 1

<small>LIVING ROOM – DAY</small>
*(Blanche, on couch, cools herself with hand fan. Sophia, on
couch, reads paper. There are christmas tree and decorations.
Rose hangs wreath on open front door, hums "Jingle Bells". She
hums through "one horse open sleigh")*

ROSE   Hey!

BLANCHE   Rose, for the past half hour you've been
humming "Jingle Bells" and yelling "Hey!"
Now, why must you do that?

ROSE   Because it's too hard to hum the "Hey!"
*(She exits to kitchen. Dorothy enters with shopping
bag)*

DOROTHY   Oh boy, it is hell out there! Oh, it must be at
least a hundred and three. And the mall was
impossible.

SOPHIA   Did you get something for the grandchildren?

DOROTHY   Oh, please. You know, Robbie wants a Batman
hat. I went to six different stores, they were all
sold out. I finally went to one store where they
had *one* hat left, and another woman saw it.
Oh, I cannot believe a person would push a
perfect stranger out of the way, step on her
hand and give her an elbow to the forehead just
for a Batman hat. But I did it anyway. I got the
hat. No, I guess I just have this thing about
giving gifts that are more fun than the ones my

grandparents used to give me. Ma, do you remember that Christmas they gave me soap in the shape of the Seven Dwarfs?

BLANCHE   Well now, what's wrong with that?

DOROTHY   Ah, what kid wants to play with soap? Besides, after a couple of baths, they looked like seven suppositories.
DOORBELL
(*Dorothy answers. It's Stan with toupée and gift*)

STAN   Hi, it's me, Stan. I brought you a gift.

DOROTHY   (*Takes gift*)
Oh, why thank you, Stanley. Oh, and look, there's a little card.
(*Reading card*)
"Merry Christmas, 'Sports Illustrated' subscriber."

STAN   (*Clears throat*)
You don't have a baseball radio, do you, Dorothy?

DOROTHY   Stanley, why are you really here?

STAN   I am going to make all you women wealthy.

DOROTHY   How come whenever my ship comes in it's leaking?

STAN   I am planning on opening a research and development lab. We can come up with new and exciting novelties that will make today's plastic vomit obsolete. To make all of this happen, all I need from each of you is a thousand dollars. What do you say?

LADIES   No!

STAN   Okay. Make it a hundred. But no monthly report.

DOROTHY   Goodbye, Stanley.

STAN	Well, why don't I just wait outside, give you a few minutes to think this over?
DOROTHY	Fine, Fine. (*Stan exits. Dorothy closes door*) If he's still here in the morning, let's give him coffee, okay?
SOPHIA	It's a nightmare. We've been visited by the yutz of Christmas past.
DOROTHY	I am drained of what little holiday spirit I had.
BLANCHE	Oh, that's too bad, because we still have to shop for presents for each other.
DOROTHY	Ah, now, wait a minute. Listen, I've been giving this a lot of thought. I mean, none of us wants to go shopping in this terrible heat; so why don't we just put names into a hat and then we just have to pick out a gift for the one person whose name we pick?
SOPHIA	There's only one problem with your plan, pussycat. One of us is gonna get the gift from Rose.
BLANCHE	Dorothy, she's right. And you know how hard it is pretending to like Rose's gifts. Uh-uh, forget it. No way.
DOROTHY	Oh, c'mon now, Blanche, don't be so childish. I mean, we each stand an equal chance of having our Christmas ruined. It's not gonna bother me if I get Rose's gift.
SOPHIA	Dorothy's right. Be a good sport. (*They all exit to kitchen*)

ACT ONE
Scene 2

KITCHEN – DAY (CONTINUOUS)
(Ladies enter to find Rose, humming "Jingle Bells")

DOROTHY   Rose, I have to tell you about Christmas. It is too hot to shop, the stores are mobbed and there are only two days left, so we've decided to draw names out of a hat. And that way each of us only has to buy one gift.

ROSE   But Dorothy, I love shopping and I love giving gifts. And besides, if we draw names out of a hat, whose names are they gonna be, anyway?

DOROTHY   The Oak Ridge Boys, Rose. *Our* names.

ROSE   Oh. Gee, I'm not sure about this. I mean, when you think about Christmas, don't you think about giving gifts?
(At table, Blanche begins writing their names on slips of paper)

DOROTHY   Yes, but that's not the first thing. You know, when I think of Christmas, I think of Christmas in New York – the decorations in Macy's window, the show at Radio City, skaters on the ice at Mitsubishi Centre . . .

SOPHIA   In the old days, on Christmas Eve, we used to go to midnight Mass.

DOROTHY   Oh.

SOPHIA   Remember, Dorothy?

DOROTHY   Sure I do. Ah, Ma, the music and the candles . . . It was beautiful.

SOPHIA   And the Mass was in Latin, a fine, old Italian language. Now, who knows? Sometimes it's in English, sometimes in Spanish. If you ask me, they should go back to Latin, the language Jesus spoke.

DOROTHY   Ma, he spoke Hebrew.

SOPHIA   Even in church?

ROSE   You know, I've been thinking.

BLANCHE   Oh, that would explain the beads of sweat.
(Blanche has placed four slips of paper into bowl on table)

ROSE   Maybe Dorothy's right. I guess I don't need a shopping spree to give me the Christmas spirit. My church is serving Christmas dinner to poor, hungry people in the neighbourhood and I volunteered to go down and help serve. That'll do the trick for me.

DOROTHY   Okay then, let's do it. C'mon, now look – remember, you only buy for the person whose name you pick.
(To Blanche)
And it doesn't matter who picks you, because it's bound to be a terrific gift. Go ahead, Blanche.

BLANCHE   *(Picks slip of paper from bowl)*
Oh, okay. Okay, I buy for . . .
(Opens it)
. . . Dorothy.

DOROTHY   Oh, yes! Yes! Yes! Yes! Oh, yes! Oh . . .

ROSE   Boy, Blanche, I didn't realize you were such a big spender.
(Blanche gives a false laugh)

SOPHIA   Go ahead, Dorothy. You go.

DOROTHY   *(Takes paper)* Okay. I buy for . . . Ma.

SOPHIA   Yes!
(They laugh heartily)

ROSE	This really *was* a good idea. This is really fun.
BLANCHE	Oh shut up, Rose.
ROSE	I-Is it m-my turn?
DOROTHY	Yeah.
ROSE	Okay. I buy for . . . *(Reaches into hat, takes paper and opens it)* . . . Rose.
BLANCHE	Oh, thank you, God!
DOROTHY	No, no, no. Rose, you can't pick yourself.
ROSE	Oh, thank goodness. I'm so hard to shop for.
DOROTHY	Rose, you buy for . . .
SOPHIA	Blanche!
ROSE	Okay, thanks, Dorothy. This really was a good idea. *(To Blanche)* I don't want to spoil the surprise, but in a couple of weeks someone in this room is gonna know how to yodel.

ACT ONE
Scene 3

LIVING ROOM – CHRISTMAS MORNING
(The four women open gifts. Sophia stares at a just-opened gift)

SOPHIA	*(To Dorothy)* Your brother Phil, God rest his brain, gives the worst presents in the world. What kind of gift is dental floss?
ROSE	Well, it's waxed and mint flavoured.
SOPHIA	*(Tosses floss to Rose)* Here, go floss yourself. This stinks. After the swell gift I sent him.

BLANCHE	What was it?
SOPHIA	A catalogue item.
BLANCHE	L.L. Bean?
SOPHIA	Victoria's Secret.
ROSE	(*Opens gift*) Here it is: my present from Kirsten. Oh, she always knows just what her mother wants. (*Takes out glass snowball, shakes it and laughs*) It's a St. Olaf snowball!
BLANCHE	Rose, there's nothin' in there but snow.
ROSE	That's what St. Olaf looks like in winter. (*Gets plate of cookies*) Who's for some fresh-baked Christmas cookies?
DOROTHY	(*Stares at cookies*) Rose, why are the Christmas cookies in the shape of American flags and liberty bells?
ROSE	I couldn't find the Christmas cookie cutters, so I used the Fourth of July cookie cutters instead.
SOPHIA	(*Holding up flag cookie*) I wonder where President Bush stands on eating the flag? (*She takes a bite of it*)
BLANCHE	Well, that's all the presents. Except for the ones we know are fruitcakes.
SOPHIA	Wait a minute. What about the present Blanche hid behind the couch?
ROSE	Oh, my gift for you! I'll get it. (*Gets gift*) Oh, I can't wait to see the look on your face.
DOROTHY	Me, too.
ROSE	(*Gives Blanche gift*) Here you go, sweetheart.

(Blanche tentatively opens it)

BLANCHE   Why, Rose, it's a beautiful blouse.

ROSE   Oh, I hope it's all right. Dorothy said you'd like something crotchless.
(Then)
Well, I'm due at church in about a half an hour. They're starting to serve Christmas dinner at one o'clock. I better get ready.

DOROTHY   Hey, Rose. Rose, could you use some extra help?

ROSE   Oh, we could use all the help we can get.

DOROTHY   Then I'm going with you.

BLANCHE   Hey, count me in. Since I didn't get a gift I have to bury out in the backyard, why, I'm feeling all Christmas-y, too.

DOROTHY   Ma? You coming?

SOPHIA   But I rented "Scarface". Oh, all right, I'll go, too. Hey, I got an idea. We got all these fruitcakes from this Christmas, last Christmas, and the Christmas before that . . . Why don't we gather them all up and . . .

DOROTHY   And, what build a bomb shelter?

SOPHIA   No. We can unload them . . . I-I mean, bring them to the church for dessert.

ROSE   Well, actually, I think that's very nice. Like we say in St. Olaf, Christmas without fruitcake is like Saint Sigmund's Day without the headless boy.
(They all head for the kitchen)

ACT ONE
Scene 4

CHURCH SOCIAL HALL – LATER THAT DAY
(Tables with folding chairs, two serving tables. Volunteers, including golden girls, prepare. No "guests" have arrived. Reverend Avery gives a talk)

REVEREND
AVERY

Well, before we open the doors, I just want to thank you all for taking time away from your own Christmas to provide Christmas for some that are less fortunate. We promise to turn away no one, remembering how Mary and Joseph were turned away at the inn.

ROSE

Reverend Avery – it's always puzzled me; why didn't Mary and Joseph call ahead for reservations? Surely they must have realized how impossible it is to get a hotel room during the Christmas season.

REVEREND
AVERY

I guess that's one for the theologians, Rose. *(He flees. Sophia enters from kitchen with pan of turkey)*

SOPHIA

I can never get used to serving turkey for Christmas dinner. It's so un-Sicilian.

BLANCHE

Well, what did you serve?

SOPHIA

Eels.

BLANCHE

Eels!?

DOROTHY

Yeah, it's true. Eels are a traditional part of a Sicilian Christmas.

SOPHIA

Of course, after Christmas it's eel croquettes, eel hash, eel tetrazzini . . .

ROSE

I sure miss a traditional St. Olaf Christmas.

DOROTHY

Uh, excuse me, Rose. Do we have time to run out and get hit by a bus?

ROSE	First there'd be the Christmas pageant with the shepherds and the angels and the two wise men.
BLANCHE	There were three wise men, Rose.
ROSE	Not in St. Olaf. Then we'd all go down to the town square and try to form a circle. And then, we'd all go home and smoke kippers.
BLANCHE	Why, Rose?
ROSE	Because it's the best way to get your house to smell like kippers. And then, in keeping with the spirit of Christmas, it was traditional to let all the animals sleep inside that night. And then the next morning, the rumours would start and they'd continue until New Year's, and we'd all make resolutions that it would never happen again. But then, the next year all it took was a little eggnog and one wise guy saying, "What the hell, it's Christmas."
	(Angle: Reverend Avery at doors)
REVEREND AVERY	All right, volunteers. Stand by. I'm opening the doors.
	(Volunteers take positions. Reverend Avery opens doors)
	Welcome! Welcome, everybody! Merry Christmas!
	(People file in. Some shabbily dressed, many not. Some children. Also, a forlorn Santa Claus)
BLANCHE	I just never thought there'd be children.
ROSE	I know. And what is Santa Claus doing here?
BLANCHE	Oh, they pay these poor out-of-work guys ten, fifteen bucks to stand on street corners ringing their bells for charitable contributions. A lot of them can't afford the price of a meal.
	(Santa Claus has cut to front of serving line. Servers put food on his tray. He reaches Dorothy)

SANTA	Hello there.
DOROTHY	Hello, Santa Claus.
SANTA	(*Removing hat and beard*) Dorothy, it's me; Stanley.

END OF ACT ONE

ACT TWO
Scene 1

CHURCH SOCIAL HALL – STILL LATER THAT DAY
(*People eating, others are being served. Rose, Blanche and Sophia, among others, serve, clear, etc. Dorothy talks to Stan, still as Santa, but without beard, cap, or toupée*)

DOROTHY	Stan, what are you doing here? What happened with the research and development deal?
STAN	Nah, that was just me trying to get some extra cash to tide me through the holidays.
DOROTHY	You mean you were gonna cheat us?
STAN	Oh, sure, if you want to label everything.
DOROTHY	Stan, how could you?
STAN	What did you want me to tell you, Dorothy? That I was broke? That I miscalculated the public taste? I thought I was gonna go through the roof with my plastic reindeer poop.
DOROTHY	That's what happens when you aim too high.
STAN	And then I figured with the drought and the danger of fires, the one novelty item that would really take off this season is a little Santa wearing sunglasses, driving a fire engine. So I put every last cent I had into that hunch and I ordered twelve gross from my supplier in Germany. Everything's getting out of East

Berlin except my fire engines. They didn't get here till last night.

DOROTHY Come on, Stanley, you've been down before. This is the nature of your business. Why don't you go home and enjoy Christmas, then face the future tomorrow?

STAN I can't go home.

DOROTHY Why not?

STAN Katherine threw me out.

DOROTHY Your wife threw you out? I had no idea she was that bright. What happened?

STAN Katherine accused me of infidelity.

DOROTHY Oh, damn it, Stan. This makes those infidelities during our marriage seem much less special.

STAN Why did this have to happen to me? Broke and homeless on Christmas. Why me?

DOROTHY (*Indicating the people eating*)
Why you? Why them? Look around you. You're not exactly alone. This is probably the only Christmas these kids are gonna have. Think about that for awhile. It might take your mind off your own self-pity. I've got to go back to work.
(*She exits to kitchen*)

STAN (*To a child, indicates Dorothy:*) Mrs. Sensitive.

ACT TWO
Scene 2

SOCIAL HALL KITCHEN ANNEX – SHORT TIME LATER
(*Blanche puts pie on plates. Dorothy helps*)

BLANCHE You know, being here reminds me of my

favourite Christmas back in 1951 which I spent at the U.S.O. making a better Christmas for our boys getting ready to leave for Korea. I gave those servicemen something even Mr. Bob Hope himself could not give them.

DOROTHY   A rash?

BLANCHE   Donuts, Dorothy. Big Daddy was part-owner of a donut shop. Did you really think this was gonna be a story about sex? This is a beautiful Christmas story, Dorothy. Now that really hurts me.

DOROTHY   Oh, I'm sorry, Blanche.

BLANCHE   Anyway, after the boys had their donuts . . . Actually, at this point it does change more into a Veteran's Day story.
(Rose and Reverend Avery enter with dirty dishes)

REVEREND AVERY   In fact, what happened to Dorothy's ex-husband is not that uncommon.

ROSE   Really?

REVEREND AVERY   Well, you'd be surprised how many people are only two or three paychecks away from being out on the street. The suddenly poor are all around us, and once you've been knocked down like that, it's very hard to recover.

DOROTHY   What's going to happen to all these people?

REVEREND AVERY   I don't know. There's no affordable housing. The rents keep going up and up and the minimum wage has been held down.

ROSE   Seems so unfair.

REVEREND AVERY   Oh, that's because it is. There are three million homeless, hungry people in this country.

BLANCHE   What bothers me is those people out there are being fed today because it's Christmas, but where do they eat tomorrow?

REVEREND
AVERY
When the Great Communicator talked about his vision of "A city on a hill", I wonder if it included people sleeping on gratings in the street?
(Sophia enters from dining area)

SOPHIA
Dorothy, Stan's out there feeling so sorry for himself he's bringing down the homeless.

DOROTHY
Uh, Blanche, will you take over for me, please?

BLANCHE
What are you gonna do?

DOROTHY
I'm gonna go and try to make Stan feel like a whole man again.

ROSE
Anything you need?

DOROTHY
Yes, half a man.
(She exits)

BLANCHE
Sophia, you were just putting me on about those eels, right?

SOPHIA
Please. In Sicily it wouldn't be Christmas without a plate of eels. Eels and larks.

BLANCHE
Larks!? Well, honey, larks aren't eating birds, they're singing birds.

SOPHIA
They don't sing long in Sicily.
(Sophia exits)

ACT TWO
Scene 3

CHURCH SOCIAL HALL – DAY (CONTINUOUS)
(Dorothy approaches Stan)

DOROTHY
Stanley?

STAN
Yeah.

(She gestures him to vestibule. They exit)
CHURCH VESTIBULE – DAY (CONTINUOUS)
(Dorothy and Stan enter)

DOROTHY   I forgot to wish you a merry Christmas.

STAN   Some Christmas.

DOROTHY   Oh, come on, Stanley, you're the most fortunate person here.

STAN   Big deal.

DOROTHY   Stanley, you've always been able to turn bad holidays around. Do you remember the Christmas we were so broke that you actually convinced the kids that Christmas was the twenty-sixth, and then you went out and got a Christmas tree from somebody's garbage? You trimmed it with gum wrappers and pull tabs, and then you turned on the television and they were playing "Jim Thorpe, All American", and you told the kids it was "King of Kings"?

STAN   And they believed it, too.

DOROTHY   Right up to the part where Jesus had his Olympic medals taken away for playing professional baseball.

STAN   That became sort of a tradition with us.

DOROTHY   Yeah. You had ingenuity then. You didn't let anything beat you. And you can do it again, Stan, if you just work hard and turn on that Zbornak charm.

STAN   I am pretty good at that.

DOROTHY   Oh, you could charm the pants off anybody. I have to believe that. Otherwise, I was easy.

STAN   But, Dorothy, it's, it's different this time. Sure, sure, I've scraped the bottom of the barrel before – but this time I don't even have a barrel!

DOROTHY	Oh, Stan, will you stop whining? It's pathetic.
STAN	That's the most effective way *to* whine! All I need is a few bucks . . . just a little seed money, I – (*Dorothy gives Stan money from purse*)
DOROTHY	Okay, okay, here, here, Stan. Take it.
STAN	Atta girl. To show you how much I love you, I'm not even gonna count it.
DOROTHY	I hate you, Stanley. You are the lowest.
STAN	I'm sorry, Dorothy, if I am no longer the man you divorced.
DOROTHY	So am I.
STAN	Well, I'd love to stick around and be belittled, but –
DOROTHY	Fine, fine. You've eaten. Go somewhere else and wallow. (*She exits to social hall, with Stan on her heels*) CHURCH SOCIAL HALL – DAY (CONTINUOUS) (*They enter. Stan gets hat, beard, then:*)
STAN	Better be careful, Dorothy. You're not the only ex-wife I have.
DOROTHY	Then why do you keep bothering me?
STAN	You're the only one who answers the door. (*He exits*)

ACT TWO
Scene 4

CHURCH SOCIAL HALL – *LATER THAT DAY*
(*Rose sings with children*)

ROSE/ CHILDREN	"FA-LA-LA-LA-LA . . . LA-LA-LA-LA." (*They cheer, then Rose joins the others*)

REVEREND AVERY	Well, I guess that about does it. All the food is gone.
SOPHIA	Except the fruitcake. I don't get it. There's more now than when we started.
BLANCHE	I just wish there was something more we could do for these people.
ROSE	Especially the children.
REVEREND AVERY	Yes, I know. I'm supposed to look after their spiritual needs, but even I can't help thinking they have other needs that are far more pressing. *(Crosses to front of room, addresses guests)* Well, I'd like to thank you all very much for coming. I wish you every blessing for the new year . . . *(Doors burst open. Santa (Stan) enters with sack)*
SANTA (STAN)	Merry Christmas! Ho, ho, ho! Here's Santa with toys for all the good boys and girls. Ho, ho, ho! *(Children, cheering, cluster around him)* Have you all been good boys and girls?
CHILDREN	Yeah!
SANTA (STAN)	Ah-ha! Ho, ho, ho! Ho, ho, ho ho, ho, ho . . .! *(He hands out fire engines with santas driving them. The children are delighted. The ladies look on with approval)*

ACT TWO
Scene 5

SOCIAL HALL KITCHEN ANNEX – STILL LATER THAT DAY
(Guests and volunteers have gone. The girls and Stan, minus toupée, beard and cap, have coffee)

DOROTHY	I'm proud of you, Stan, really proud.

BLANCHE   That was a lovely thing you did.

DOROTHY   You made me believe in Santa Claus again.

SOPHIA   Me, too.

ROSE   Oh, not me. I knew it was Stan all along.

STAN   After I walked out of here this afternoon, I realized that I'm more fortunate than a lot of people. Tomorrow I'm gonna get the jump on the Easter season. I have a new idea for a great novelty – it's a decorated Easter egg with a little window in it. And when you look into it, you see a beautiful Easter scene.

BLANCHE   Well, that's not a new idea. Those Easter eggs have been around for years and years.

STAN   Yes. But this one leaves a black circle around your eyes!

DOROTHY   That practically screams "Easter".

STAN   And you know, Dorothy, I apologized to my wife, and in the spirit of Christmas, she's letting me come back home.

DOROTHY   Great. In that case, you can give me back the sixty dollars I gave you.

STAN   Well, when I apologized, I said it with flowers.

DOROTHY   What, sixty dollars worth?

STAN   Dorothy, I may be a lot of things, but I'm not cheap.
             (*He exits*)

DOROTHY   You know, actually this is one of the best Christmases I ever spent with Stan.

SOPHIA   It was pretty nice.

BLANCHE   I can't remember feeling this proud of myself so early in this evening.

DOROTHY   No, we did good.

ROSE   Just wish we could do more.

DOROTHY   Oh, so do I. I mean, we have a place to go
              home to, and so many people don't. We should
              keep them in our hearts and our minds not just
              at Christmas, but every day of the year.

SOPHIA   It's more than a place to go. It's having
              someone there for you. We have each other.
              There's always someone there.

DOROTHY   That's right.

BLANCHE   That's right, darling. So, let's go home. Ha!
              (They start for door)

ROSE   Thanks, girls, for coming down and helping
              out.
              (Dorothy, Blanche and rose all speak at once)

DOROTHY   Oh, thank you for having us, Rose.

ROSE   Oh . . .

BLANCHE   Oh, it was wonderful. I'm glad you asked.

ROSE   And hey – merry Christmas!
              (As they group hug, they talk simultaneously)

BLANCHE   Oh, merry, merry Christmas!

DOROTHY   Oh, merry Christmas! Ah . . .

SOPHIA   Merry Christmas . . .
              END OF ACT TWO

LIKE THE BEEP BEEP BEEP OF THE TOM – TOM

Written by: PHILIP JAYSON LASKER
Directed by: TERRY HUGHES

· *Introduction* ·

CONCERN ABOUT HEALTH, and the nagging insecurity it can produce, is the theme which unites the friends round Blanche. Blanche, normally so much in the pink that she may have more cause to worry about the health of her numerous boyfriends, arrives home to announce that she is wearing a device which will monitor her heartbeat. Typically she loads the statement with wit:

"Dr Stein just thought my heart sounded a little ... irregular. I think it's 'cause I was so uncomfortable sitting there topless with a strange man."

Refreshingly odd as, unusually for Blanche, her light flirtatious joking is replaced by anxious introspection; Blanche decides to follow the doctor's instructions and so manages to transcend even Sophia's poison darts.

Blanche: "He wants to match the heartbeat that this records to my activities, so for the next 24 hours I have to write down everything I do."

Sophia: And you're not embarassed to have him read that smut?"

Finally, learning from the doctor that "he wants to put a pacemaker in me" (Sophia – "Everybody's got a nickname for it"), she's seized by panic and realises that age is staring her in the face:

"I just want to be young and beautiful and healthy again."

However, even in her hospital bed, vanity refuses to take a back seat. As the operation for the insertion of the pacemaker nears, Blanche is frantic that she will be left with a scar, albeit a tiny one. Her next encounter with boyfriend Simon reveals an unfamiliar Blanche who is scared to make love while kitted out with a pacemaker.

Blanche: "But this is in me. Oh, Simon, for the first time in my life, I'm just scared of intimacy."

Blanche's condition, and her normal sexual appetite, are an excuse to wheel on plenty of wisecracking humour at her expense. While Sophia asserts that "she'll be up and back on her back in no time", Dorothy realises that Blanche has been manless for two weeks since "all the pictures on my wall are straight".

Untypically forced to look beyond the next pair of trousers for the meaning of life, Blanche, claiming that she has not only had an out-of-body experience but is also renouncing sex, sinks into thought:

"I've had a life-altering experience, Simon. I need time to think. To gather my priorities and put 'em all in perspective."

In an apt sub-text, Rose, who suggests that Blanche sing a wartime song to conquer fear, continues the theme of health as she toys with some weight-loss products which she has to test for work. Vacuum Slacks and Electric Muscle Stimulators maintain the concern with health while also providing a foil for Blanche's anxious intensity.

CAST
DOROTHY, ROSE, BLANCHE, SOPHIA, SIMON, DR STEIN,
ORDERLY.

ACT ONE
Scene 1

LANAI – AFTERNOON
(Sophia on chaise, deep in thought, Dorothy enters)

DOROTHY   Hi, Ma, whatcha doing?

SOPHIA   Thinking.

DOROTHY   About what?

SOPHIA   About wind . . . water . . . rocks . . . Man's place in the delicate balance of nature's harmony . . . Where we're going . . . Where the road ends.

DOROTHY   Gee, Ma. I never knew you were so philosophical.

SOPHIA   I'm not. It's those damn Infiniti commercials. They're driving me crazy.

ROSE   (O.C.) Hello? Where is everybody?

DOROTHY   Uh, we're out here, Rose.
(Rose enters, laden with packages)

ROSE   Hi.

DOROTHY   What's all that?

ROSE   Weight loss products I have to test for work. You wouldn't believe the length people go to just to drop a few pounds. I heard about one woman who even had her jaw wired shut.

DOROTHY   Oh, is that something that you'll be testing, Rose?
(Blanche enters, wearing light jacket)

BLANCHE   Ohh, here you all are.

DOROTHY	How'd your physical go?
BLANCHE	Oh, just fine. The doctor could not believe it when I told him my age.
DOROTHY	Why, what age did you tell him? *(Blanche removes jacket. She's wearing halter monitor)* Blanche, what is that thing?
SOPHIA	She's decided to install a change machine.
BLANCHE	Oh, it's um, it's called a halter monitor. Makes a kinda ticker tape of the heart.
ROSE	What's wrong with your heart?
BLANCHE	Oh, nothing. Dr. Stein just thought it sounded a little – irregular. I think it's 'cause I was so uncomfortable sitting there topless with a strange man.
DOROTHY	Next time, just pretend you're at home and he's the bug guy.
ROSE	Blanche, what did the doctor say?
BLANCHE	Oh – he just muttered something in Latin. I explained to him that Simon and I have been going out every night – and it's just fatigue.
DOROTHY	And then what did he say?
BLANCHE	He wants to match the heartbeats that this records to my activities, so for the next twenty-four hours I have to write down everything I do.
SOPHIA	And you're not embarrassed to have him read that smut?
DOROTHY	I'm proud of you, Blanche. Boy, if this were me, I would be really scared.
ROSE	When I'm scared I put my head between my knees.

DOROTHY   No, that's for nausea.

ROSE   When I'm scared I'm nauseous. You remember what happened when that man tried to steal my purse?

DOROTHY   Worked better than mace.
(*To Blanche*)
Honey, I'm, sure there's nothing to worry about.

BLANCHE   Well, anyway, all the same, I'd better get busy writing down my activities. And I'd better call Simon to cancel our date for tonight. You know, I'm really starting to care about him, and I wouldn't want him worrying about my recording his performance. You know how fragile men's egos are. One little thing like screaming out the wrong name and they go all to pieces.
(*Blanche exits*)

ACT ONE
Scene 2

LIVING ROOM – NEXT AFTERNOON
(*Rose is there, hooking up her vacuum-slacks, as Dorothy enters*)

DOROTHY   Nice pants, Rose.

ROSE   They're called "Vacuum-Slacks". It's supposed to inhale all the fat from your body. Watch.
(*Hooking up to the vacuum, Rose's pants fill with air. She turns it off*)
I must've done it wrong. Maybe I oughta put it on "suck".
(*Blanche enters front door*)

BLANCHE   Oh, hello, ladies.

DOROTHY	What'd the doctor say?
BLANCHE	Oh-hoh, bad news.
DOROTHY	Oh, what?
BLANCHE	Oh, he told me he was married.
DOROTHY	Besides that, Blanche!
BLANCHE	Oh, well, puh – he was a little concerned because my pulse was slow and misbehaving – *(Noticing)* Rose, those pants . . . not with those shoes.
DOROTHY	Blanche, the doctor.
BLANCHE	Oh, you know how they get over the slightest little thing.
DOROTHY	And – ?
BLANCHE	Oh, and Dr. Worrywart wants me to check into the hospital for more tests. *(Sophia enters)*
SOPHIA	Dorothy, have you been fooling around with my Tip O'Neill calendar?
DOROTHY	Uh, no, Ma, I haven't.
SOPHIA	Come on, I'm missing March. It's the month where he's playing volleyball with Jesse Helms.
DOROTHY	Ma, not now. Blanche's doctor wants her to go back to the hospital for more tests.
ROSE	It makes sense. Just to be on the safe side.
DOROTHY	Oh, well of course it does. I mean, what kind of a doctor would he be if he didn't want to check out everything?
BLANCHE	Yeah, well – if it makes him happy. If everything's as bad as he thinks it is – he wants to put a pacemaker in me?
SOPHIA	Everybody's got a nickname for it.

BLANCHE	I don't think I've ever been so scared in all my life!
ROSE	You know what I do when I'm scared?
SOPHIA	You toss your cookies.
ROSE	I mean besides that. I sing.
DOROTHY	You what?
ROSE	A lullaby my mother used to sing to me when I was a little girl. So when I'm scared or alone, I sing it, and it gives me courage.
BLANCHE	No song is gonna help me! (*Blanche begins to cry. A few beats. Finally Rose sings*)
ROSE	"OVER THERE, OVER THERE . . . SEND THE WORD SEND THE WORD OVER THERE . . . THAT THE YANKS ARE COMING, THE YANKS ARE COMING –"
DOROTHY	That is the lullaby that your mother sang to you?
ROSE	Well, it's the only song she knew. During World War I she gave out doughnuts and coffee to the doughboys before they boarded the trains for Europe. It works – truly! She said no one can be scared when they hear that song – except maybe the Kaiser!
BLANCHE	I don't need a song! I just want to be young and beautiful and healthy again!
DOROTHY	Blanche, that's what we all want.
BLANCHE	I know – but I deserve it!

ACT ONE
Scene 3

HOSPITAL ROOM – DAY (A WEEK LATER)
(Blanche sits up in bed, puts on make-up. Doctor Stein enters)

DOCTOR STEIN   How're we feeling, Mrs Devereaux?

BLANCHE   A little nervous.

DOCTOR STEIN   Eh-you really don't need make-up.

BLANCHE   Well, I wanna look good – just in case.

DOCTOR STEIN   Just in case what?

BLANCHE   In case something should go wrong – I've been to enough funerals to see how they make up dead people! They look like clowns! You expect to see a dozen of 'em jump out of one coffin!

DOCTOR STEIN   Well, nothing will go wrong. I've done this procedure a hundred times. You'll be fine in a week. All we do is cut a small incision below the collarbone, make a little pocket for the pacemaker under this muscle, then feed a tiny wire through the vein and into the heart. Then the pacemaker gives little electric shocks to the valve which regulates the heartbeat.

BLANCHE   You mean you're going to cut into me?

DOCTOR STEIN   You did know that.

BLANCHE   Won't that leave a scar?

DOCTOR STEIN   Two inches, tops.

BLANCHE   Oh, I'm sorry. But I can't have any scars. See,

my clothes are all off-the-shoulder – sooner or later. Sorry, I have to give this some more thought.
(Dorothy, Rose, and Sophia enter)

DOCTOR STEIN N-n-n-no we don't have time for that. Now, everybody's already washed their hands. Believe me – it'll be alright.
(Dorothy, Rose and Sophia enter. Doctor Stein starts to exit)

DOROTHY *(Stops him)*
What, is anything wrong?

DOCTOR STEIN Eh, she just realized there's going to be a scar. It's really just last minute stage fright. All my patients have it.
(He exits)

DOROTHY Oh, honey, I'm sure it'll be nothing. You'll hardly notice it.

BLANCHE That madman wants to rip me open from stem to stern!

SOPHIA Your two favourite parts!
(Two orderlies enter with Gurney)

ORDERLY 1 Are we ready?

BLANCHE I reckon so.
(Blanche gets on Gurney)
How do I look?

DOROTHY They won't be able to take their eyes off you.
(Blanche laughs nervously. Orderlies wheel her out. As she looks back at girls:)

ROSE "OVER THERE . . .

ROSE/ DOROTHY/ SOPHIA OVER THERE . . .
SEND THE WORD
SEND THE WORD
OVER THERE . . .

THAT THE YANKS ARE COMING . . .
THE YANKS ARE COMING . . .
(A *patient, a man in his eighties, passes by, salutes*)
THE DRUMS RUM-TUMMING
EVERYWHERE . . .
SAY A PRAYER . . .
SAY A PRAYER . . .
SEND THE WORD
SEND THE WORD
TO BEWARE . . .
WE'RE COMING . . ."
END OF ACT ONE

ACT TWO
Scene 1

KITCHEN – NIGHT (A WEEK LATER)
(*Rose and Dorothy at table. Sophia enters with tray*)

DOROTHY How's Blanche?

SOPHIA She's fine. She'll be up and back on her back in no time.

ROSE Sophia, it's been wonderful watching you take care of Blanche all week.

SOPHIA I feel like a regular hospital worker.

ROSE Haah, that's nice.

SOPHIA Yeah. I just took all the money and jewelery out of her nightstand.
(*Dorothy shoots her a look. Sophia looks in cabinet*)
Hey, where's my microwave popcorn?

ROSE We gave it away. Since Blanche got her pacemaker, the doctor says we can't use the microwave.

SOPHIA But I love that popcorn.

DOROTHY   Ma, if we use the microwave, Blanche could die.

SOPHIA   Same thing with Cup O'Noodles?

DOROTHY   We're not going to use it, Ma. As a matter of fact, tomorrow the people from Goodwill are coming to pick it up.

SOPHIA   But I love this microwave. I'm eighty-three years old. D'you want me to spend what little time I have left waiting for a baked potato? (*Blanche enters*)

BLANCHE   Where's my money, old woman?

SOPHIA   I knew that would get her up. I was born to heal. Here's your money and your high school ring.
(*Reading*)
Class of ninet –

BLANCHE   (*Grabbing it*) Give me that.

ROSE   Oh, Blanche, it's good to see you back to your old self again. But don't forget, the doctor said nothing strenuous for a few days, then you'll be fine.

BLANCHE   I am not back to my old self. As a matter of fact, I may never be.

DOROTHY   What are you talking about, Blanche?

BLANCHE   Listen, I know this sounds crazy, and if it hadn't happened to me I wouldn't believe it either, but while I was being operated on, I had an out-of-body experience! I was . . . floating . . . looking down at myself I-It was like . . . It was like . . .

DOROTHY   What, the mirror on your bedroom ceiling?

BLANCHE   . . . It was like I was my own conscience! That's when I knew things were different.

DOROTHY	Different how?
BLANCHE	I was in that grey area between life and death. Uh-uh, the time has come for me to reevaluate my life. For me to take stock of myself. I just know that there's a part of me that nobody's ever seen.
SOPHIA	I find that hard to believe.
BLANCHE	If a five-thousand-year-old Indian shows up, tell him I want to know more about his people. *(Blanche exits)*
SOPHIA	For this we're giving up Cheez-Whiz nachos?

ACT TWO
Scene 2

LIVING ROOM – NIGHT (TWO WEEKS LATER)
(Dorothy on couch, reading. Sophia reads TV listing)

SOPHIA	Hey, Dorothy, guess who's on Johnny Carson tonight?
DOROTHY	Who?
SOPHIA	Johnny Carson!
DOROTHY	Must be the anniversary show. *(Rose enters – hooked up to electric muscle stimulator with little sensors on thighs, arms)*
DOROTHY	Rose, what's that supposed to be?
ROSE	A flab stimulator. You hook these things to your muscles, they give out an electric charge, and help get rid of unwanted fat deposits.
SOPHIA	Does it come in a hat?
ROSE	Where's Blanche?
DOROTHY	Oh, she's out on a date with Simon. It's her first time out, so who knows when she'll be home?

SOPHIA   Checkout time is usually noon.

DOROTHY   You know, Blanche has been without a date for weeks. I know that because all the pictures on my wall are straight.

SOPHIA   Hey, it's never easy to go without. I remember when my mother-in-law came to stay with Sal and me when we were first married. For two months, Dorothy, your father and I didn't have sex.

DOROTHY   Why not, Ma?

SOPHIA   She slept in between us. It was a very small place. Have you ever seen an Italian after he's gone without?

DOROTHY   No.

SOPHIA   That's because your father was the only one.

ROSE   Well she finally left, didn't she, Sophia?

SOPHIA   Yeah. I'll never forget that day. Your father stayed home from work.
(Dorothy chuckles)
Unfortunately, I couldn't get the day off. I don't know what he did, but he was happy when I got home.

ROSE   Since Charlie was a travelling salesman, sometimes I'd be alone for weeks. I used to have so much trouble sleeping I tried counting sheep.

DOROTHY   Rose, if there are real sheep in this story, I do not want to hear it.

ROSE   Okay.
(Blanche enters front door with Simon. All ad-lib hellos)

BLANCHE   Ahah, hi.

DOROTHY   Ohhh, Simon, good to see you again. How
           have you been?

SIMON   A little lonely.
           (Putting an arm around Blanche)
           But I'm better now.

ROSE   Ahh, that's sweet.

SIMON   I can not believe how much I've missed this
           little girl.

SOPHIA   *(To Dorothy)*
           This guy is growing antlers.

BLANCHE   I guess I'd better say good night.
           *(Blanche takes Simon onto porch, leaving door
           open)*
           PORCH – NIGHT (CONTINUOUS)

BLANCHE   Uhuh, I had a very nice time.

SIMON   You mean, eh, our date is over?

BLANCHE   Well, we went to dinner and a movie. Why,
           what's left?

SIMON   I never know.

BLANCHE   I'm sorry. I-I'm-I'm just not ready yet. You
           understand.

SIMON   Of course – as long as that's my only choice.

BLANCHE   I've had a life-altering experience, Simon. I
           need time to think. To gather my priorities and
           put 'em all in perspective.

SIMON   Whatever you need. I'll call you tomorrow?

BLANCHE   Sure.
           *(Simon goes to kiss her. She turns her face so the
           kiss lands on her cheek)*
           (Nervous laugh)
           You're not upset, are you?

SIMON   No, no, no. Boy, what a beautiful night. Think

I'll push the car home.
(He exits. Blanche exits to living room)

LIVING ROOM – (CONTINUOUS)
(Blanche enters. The ladies are there as before)

ROSE   Your date is over?

BLANCHE   You sound surprised.

DOROTHY   Well, it's just that your dates usually end with a
            little – pillow talk.

SOPHIA   Yeah, like, "What did you say your name was
            again?"

BLANCHE   I would've expected my three best friends to
            understand. That I'm just not ready yet!

ROSE   But, Blanche, the doctor said you could do
            everything you did before.

BLANCHE   That's all very well for him to say. The doctor's
            not me.

DOROTHY   Blanche, what are you saying?

BLANCHE   I've made a decision. Blanche Devereaux is
            giving up sex.
            (She exits to hallway)

SOPHIA   And what does that do to the morale of our
            boys overseas?

ACT TWO
Scene 3

KITCHEN – MORNING (TWO WEEKS LATER)
(Dorothy and Sophia are there. Rose enters)

ROSE   Good news, girls! I've gained four pounds!

DOROTHY   How is that good news?

ROSE   Well, it means that all those weight loss

products don't work. Now to lose those four pounds I guess I'll have to go on a sensible diet that I know gets results: the St. Olaf "I can't believe this is cheese" diet.

DOROTHY   How does it work?

ROSE   You eat nothing but rice.
(Blanche enters)

BLANCHE   Good morning, ladies.
(Hands out items)
Dorothy, a popsicle stick purse for you. Sophia, a popsicle stick pot pourri box. And for you, Rose, two lovely popsicle stick earrings.

DOROTHY   So, Blanche, how are we enjoying our celibacy?

BLANCHE   Uh, just let me get a popsicle, I'll be right with you.
(Gets popsicle from freezer)

ROSE   Blanche, I'm worried. That's all you've been living on for two weeks.

BLANCHE   Well, if I don't eat the popsicle, how am I going to get to the stick?

DOROTHY   I'm glad you found a hobby, but, uh, I don't think Blanche Devereaux is going to be happy making things out of popsicle sticks instead of making love.

BLANCHE   Oh, I don't care about that anymore. I don't care about anything anymore. Life has no meaning.

SOPHIA   So, who's for popcorn?

BLANCHE   I don't know what to expect of myself with this thing in me. I just keep remembering how you're not supposed to overload electrical outlets.

ROSE   Maybe you just shouldn't make love when

you're wet.

BLANCHE   It was not an easy decision, but it's best that I retire from the sexual arena undefeated. Time I hung up my gloves.

ROSE   Gloves? Boy, you do practice safe sex!

BLANCHE   Sex is only good when your heart is in it – and that's the one organ I can't count on.

DOROTHY   Oh, now, come on, Blanche. You don't know that. But listen, if that's the way you feel, maybe you should tell Simon so that he'll know where he stands.

SOPHIA   For the last two weeks he's been standing with his legs crossed.

BLANCHE   I will. I'll tell him tonight.
(Blanche exits)

DOROTHY   I can't believe it. Blanche has gone without for two weeks. I mean, that's like Raymond Burr saying, "No gravy".

ROSE   What do you think's the matter with her?

SOPHIA   Maybe when she had that out-of-body experience she didn't get back in all the way.
(Sees their looks)
Try to discuss science with kids.

ACT TWO
Scene 4

LIVING ROOM – THAT NIGHT
(Blanche and Simon enter from front door)

BLANCHE   Um, I want to thank you for a lovely evening.

SIMON   I didn't think you noticed. You hardly said a word all evening.

(*Looking around*)
Where are the other girls?

BLANCHE Oh, they all went out to a movie. Uh, Simon, that's why I wanted to come back here. I-I wanted us to be alone.

SIMON "Oooh baby."

BLANCHE Um, here. I don't really know how to say this. I never thought I'd ever be saying this in my wildest dreams – and you know just how wild they can get. What I'm trying to tell you, Simon, the last time we made love – was the last time. Guess it's just a lucky thing that we took those snapshots.

SIMON What are you talking about?

BLANCHE I am giving up the physical side of my life. After what I've been through, I can not trust myself to climb the heights of passion anymore 'cause I can't be sure of ever getting back again.

SIMON I know you have to be concerned about the pacemaker.

BLANCHE Wouldn't you be?

SIMON Blanche, everyone I know over fifty –
(*Sees her look*)
– over forty has a pacemaker. They all lead perfectly normal lives. In every way, Blanche.

BLANCHE But this is in *me*! Oh, Simon, for the first time in my life, I'm, I'm just scared of intimacy.

SIMON Maybe this is my fault. Maybe I've been pushing you.

BLANCHE It's not you.

SIMON Blanche, you're the same person that you always were – you have to believe that.

BLANCHE	Oh, I-I want to, Simon. And I have tried. But I can't. *(Goes to front door and opens it)*
SIMON	Darlin', this is not the time for your vivid imagination to give out on us.
BLANCHE	Goodbye, Simon.
SIMON	Uuhhh, well, if you're going to kiss me off – I want my kiss. *(The kiss becomes a real lip swallower. Behind his back, she checks her pulse, kicks the door shut)* Are you all right?
BLANCHE	*(Putting her hand over her heart)* I think so. I don't feel any sparks.
SIMON	Well, in this instance I'll take that as a compliment.
BLANCHE	I am a little hot – but it's nothing I can't handle.
SIMON	What did you expect to happen?
BLANCHE	I don't know. I ju-I just kept seeing those cartoon characters with smoke coming outta their ears.
SIMON	I don't see anything.
BLANCHE	*(Starts leading him to bedroom)* Listen, there's a great big ol' television set back in my bedroom. What do you say we go in there and . . . turn it off. Long as you understand I can't make any promises.
SIMON	If you'll be brave, I'll be brave. *(They exit to hallway. Moments later, Dorothy, Rose, and Sophia enter from front door)*
DOROTHY	Ma, I said I was sorry.
SOPHIA	The least you can do when we're going to see a

	movie is say it's a foreign film.
DOROTHY	What is the big deal?
SOPHIA	I had to stand in front of the screen just to read the subtitles. And all that running back and forth to complete a sentence almost killed me!
ROSE	Wasn't that Simon's car parked out front?
DOROTHY	Are you sure? *(Goes to kitchen, calls out)* Blanche – ? *(Then)* She's not in here.
ROSE	Well, maybe she had trouble with her pacemaker and since we weren't here she called him.
DOROTHY	Oh, my God! *(The girls rush down hallway, approaching Blanche's bedroom. Dorothy puts her hand on doorknob, then, they hear Blanche from inside)*
BLANCHE	*(Sings)* "OVER THERE, OVER THERE . . ." *(Stops)* No, I said over there! *(Sings)* "SEND THE WORD SEND THE WORD OVER THERE . . . END OF ACT TWO

72
HOURS

Written by: TRACY GAMBLE &
RICHARD VACZY
Directed by: TERRY HUGHES

· *Introduction* ·

NEVER AFRAID TO grapple with serious issues, while always hitting a lighter note as well, *The Golden Girls'* scriptwriters (here Tracy Gamble and Richard Vaczy) introduce the troublesome subject of AIDS.

Just by turning Rose into a possible victim (she had a blood transfusion six years before), the writers clearly dent the common prejudice that AIDS is the exclusive province of sexually-active gays. Rose, prim, celibate and moral-minded to the last is, in her own words, a lifelong "goody-two-shoes". As an angelic youngster in her beloved St Olaf she even voted herself "the town's dumbest virgin".

After some frivolous banter about throwing out organs after surgery, our laughter grinds to a halt as the subject of AIDS is introduced in typical summary fashion:

Dorothy: "The hospital thinks the blood m-may have contained HIV antibodies."

Rose: "HIV-V – wait a minute. You're talking about AIDS? Oh well, th-this has to be some kind of mistake."

After enduring the AIDS test, Rose's customary nervi-ness gives way to frozen panic as she sits out 72 hours while awaiting the result. She finds an unlikely companion in Blanche who, for once, unhooks herself from her own self-absorption to lend support.

Blanche: "Well, I just had the test. And then I-I had a nice long talk with myself about being with so many men. And now when I am with a man I know his complete history, and we take all the necessary precautions. I just wanted you to know I understand this is not an easy time."

As this speech reveals, the writers do not stint when it comes to providing the viewer with hard facts about a subject which can so easily be distorted by the public's prejudice.

Dorothy, wishing parents would talk seriously to their kids about sex, slaps her mother down for being afraid to share both toilet and coffee cups with the beleaguered Rose. Having made an amusing aside about "using the bathroom down at the Shell station", Sophia is confronted by Dorothy who, referring to her mother's "ignorant paranoia", insists that "it's attitudes like that that add to the panic about this."

As Rose's impatience, anger and despair become a bubble fit to burst ("you're not going to want to be around me"), it is Blanche who drinks to Rose and the love they all have for her and causes Sophia to see sense and drink from any cup.

Blanche: "Listen, we're the only family Rose has here so we have to help her through whatever she's going through."

Dorothy's well-meaning campaign to Save The Wetlands is thus not only thrown into perspective but also offers some necessary light relief, while even the subject of AIDS is allowed an influx of humour.

Sophia (talking to Dorothy): "Well, maybe I used to be old-fashioned but times have changed. So when I was at the pharmacy I bought you some condoms. Your boyfriends are supposed to put them you know w-h-e-r-e."

CAST

DOROTHY, ROSE, BLANCHE, SOPHIA, DOCTOR,
RECEPTIONIST.

ACT ONE
Scene 1

KITCHEN – MORNING
(Blanche and Sophia are there. Dorothy enters, very testy)

DOROTHY   What an idiot! Of all the lamebrain, moronic dopes. I mean, if ever I wanted to reach right through the phone and strangle somebody . . .

SOPHIA   Not really a morning person, are you, pussycat?

DOROTHY   It's that caterer that I hired for my "Save the Wetlands" banquet. He's a week late with the menu, now he tells me that he's going to serve wild duck and crayfish. They come from the wetlands. It's like holding a "Save the Whales" function on a Japanese trawler.

SOPHIA   Is there an open bar?

DOROTHY   You know, Ma, that's part of the problem. Nobody cares. Do you realize what would happen if there were no swamps?

SOPHIA   New Jersey wouldn't have a state smell?

DOROTHY   I'm just in over my head. I mean, what with the banquet, press releases, petitions to be signed. Ma, what am I going to do?

BLANCHE   I'll help.

DOROTHY   Ah, Blanche, that's sweet. But, honey, aren't your hands tied with all the work that you're doing for . . . you?

BLANCHE   I know I'm not always the first one to

volunteer, but I happen to have an affection for bayous. Matter of fact, I became a woman in one.

SOPHIA   I thought you lost it in a hot air balloon.

DOROTHY   I thought you lost it at a pancake breakfast.

BLANCHE   Well, those don't count. I mean, they did at the time. But this is the definitive "where I lost my virginity" story.

SOPHIA   *(Rises)*
It's really nice of you to share something so personal with us, Blanche. In a bayou? You slut.
(She exits. Rose enters with mail)

ROSE   Mail call.

DOROTHY   Oh –

BLANCHE   *(Simultaneous with Dorothy)* Oh.

DOROTHY   – Rose you're here. That's good. I am absolutely snowed under with this wetlands thing. And, as usual, I know I can count on you.

ROSE   I'm sorry, Dorothy.

DOROTHY   What? But, Rose, you always help out with these things. You're involved in all the charities. You sent a contribution to "Save the Rich."

ROSE   I have charity work burnout, Dorothy. In the last three months I have helped with so many raffles and bake sales and car washes I have to draw the line.

DOROTHY   Well, I guess I'll manage somehow.

BLANCHE   *(Notices Rose absorbed in letter)*
What is it, Rose? Is something wrong?

ROSE   I'm not sure. St. Luke's Hospital wants me to

come in for some kind of test. Eh, that's where I
had my gallbladder out six years ago.

DOROTHY   Can I see it, Rose?

ROSE   They throw organs out after surgery.

DOROTHY   The letter, Rose.

ROSE   Oh.
          (*Hands it to Dorothy*)

DOROTHY   Mmm-hmm, seems you had a transfusion while
          you were there. The hospital thinks the blood
          m-may have contained HIV antibodies.

ROSE   HIV-wait a minute. You're talking about
          AIDS. Oh, well, th-this has to be some kind of
          a mistake.

DOROTHY   Honey, don't panic. There's just a possibility.
          This is a precaution.

ROSE   What do I do?

BLANCHE   We just call up the hospital and make an
          appointment. Everything'll be fine.

ROSE   You think so?

BLANCHE   Why I'm sure of it. Now let's plan Dorothy's
          fund-raiser. Hey, I know what would be fun.

DOROTHY   Uh, Blanche, we're going to try to raise all the
          money in one night.

BLANCHE   I know.

ACT ONE
Scene 2

LIVING ROOM – DAY (TWO DAYS LATER)
(*Dorothy is on phone. Sophia is there*)

DOROTHY   (*Into phone*)
          Yes, but this is very import – Yes, yes, I

understand . . . I understand.
(*Hangs up. Blanche enters*)

BLANCHE   Oh boy, some people.

DOROTHY   What's wrong, Blanche?

BLANCHE   Oh, Dorothy, nobody gives a damn about this "Save the Wetlands" thing. I sat in that booth of ours at the mall for three hours, not one soul came by and asked for information. What we need is some kind of swamp gimmick – like "Guess how many leeches are in the jar."

DOROTHY   I don't think so, Blanche.

BLANCHE   All right then. All right. How about a celebrity auction?

SOPHIA   Hey, if you could buy a celebrity at an auction, I'd be showering every morning with Trini Lopez.

DOROTHY   Ma, I didn't know you liked Trini Lopez.

SOPHIA   I don't. But who can I afford on a fixed income?

BLANCHE   You don't understand, Sophia. A celebrity auction is where famous people donate personal items to bid on for charities.

DOROTHY   Yeah, I mean, that's a great idea, Blanche, but it's a little late. I mean, how are we going to find celebrities to donate stuff and donate it fast?

BLANCHE   Well, I can pull some strings. It so happens I know some famous people.

DOROTHY   Who?

BLANCHE   Well, I don't want to divulge his name, but I'll give you a clue – I know what the "F" stands for in William F. Buckley.
(*Rose enters*)

ROSE   Does someone want to drive me to the hospital?

BLANCHE   Your appointment's not for three hours.

ROSE   Well, I'd like to get there early, but if you don't want to take me, I'll go without you. I might as well get used to being by myself.

BLANCHE   What does that mean?

ROSE   Well, come on. If that test turns out to be positive, you're not going to want to be around me. You or Miles or anybody.

DOROTHY   Now that is not true. And I'm sure Miles'll feel the same way.

ROSE   How am I going to tell him?

DOROTHY   You don't have to tell him anything now. You're just going for a test.

ROSE   It's not just *a* test, Dorothy.

SOPHIA¯   I know just how you feel. I remember how nervous and scared and panicked I was when I went to that neurologist to have my memory tested.

ROSE   How did you handle it?

SOPHIA   Well, usually I add a cup of bleach.

ACT ONE

Scene 3

Hospital Lab Waiting Room - Later That Day
(*Rose, Dorothy and Blanche enter and approach receptionist*)

RECEPTION- Can I help you?
IST

ROSE   I think so. I have a two o'clock appointment for an . . . AIDS blood test. My name is . . .

(*Looks at people in earshot; whispers*)
Well, it's . . .

RECEPTION-You know, we encourage anonymity, so if you'd
IST   like to give us a fictitious name for our files . . .?

ROSE   Oh, that'd be great.
(*Thinks*)
Dorothy Zbornak.
(*Dorothy reacts*)

RECEPTION-Fine. We'll call you and you'll be seeing a
I3T   counsellor and then the doctor. Meanwhile,
just take a seat, Ms . . .?

ROSE   Zbornak. Dorothy Zbornak. Z-b-o . . .

DOROTHY Let's go, Dorothy.
(*Dorothy, Blanche and Rose sit*)

ROSE   Boy, this is creepy. I mean, fake names?

BLANCHE Well, honey, it makes sense. People who test
positive have trouble getting insurance, jobs
. . . It's terrible.

ROSE   Well, the whole process is terrible. I wish it
were over.

BLANCHE It will be soon.

ROSE   I haven't been this scared since 1952 when St.
Olaf's most active volcano threatened to erupt.
Well, luckily there were some Druid priests
who were in town for the opening of
Stonehengeland. They said they could stop it if
they could sacrifice the town's dumbest virgin. I
don't know why I raised my hand. It must have
just been the excitement of the moment. But
they said the only way to prevent the eruption
was for me to crawl through their legs up the
volcano while they gave me my birthday
whacks. Well, and you're not going to believe

this, it turns out they weren't Druid priests at
all. Just a bunch of Shriners looking for a good
time.

DOROTHY It's a scary story, Rose.

ROSE W-Why don't they call me? I want to get this
over and go home.

BLANCHE Rose, come here, honey. Come here, we need
to talk.
(Takes her aside)

ROSE What, Blanche?

BLANCHE We-this is the kind of thing I tend to keep to
myself, but I want you to know – I got tested,
too. So I know what you're going through.

ROSE W-What'd you do?

BLANCHE Well, I just had the test. And then I-I had a
nice long talk with myself about being with so
many men. And now when I'm with a man I
know his complete history, and we take all the
necessary precautions. I just wanted you to
know I understand this is not an easy time.

ROSE Thank you, Blanche.
(Receptionist comes forward)

RECEPTION- Mrs. Zbornak?
IST

ROSE Dorothy Zbornak?

DOROTHY Rose!

ROSE Well, this is it.

BLANCHE All right, darling, come on. I'll go with you.
*(Blanche takes Rose's hand and they go inside
together. Sophia enters)*

SOPHIA Dorothy?

DOROTHY Ma, where have you been?

SOPHIA   I always think it's nice when you're in a hospital to walk around and cheer people up.

DOROTHY   Ah, that's nice, Ma.

SOPHIA   So after I had my prescription filled, I went up to geriatrics and sang "Anything You Can Do, I Can Do Better".

DOROTHY   Ma!

SOPHIA   What a tough crowd. They threw jello at me – if you can call that throwing. What are you reading?

DOROTHY   This pamphlet on AIDS and teenagers. It's really so discouraging. Parents don't talk to their kids about sex. I mean, this is so important you'd think they could get past their embarrassment.

SOPHIA   Thank God I was one of those progressive parents.

DOROTHY   Ah, I was amazed at how you used those technical terms. You told me never to let a boy touch me "you know where". And you spelled "where".

SOPHIA   Well, maybe I used to be old-fashioned, but times have changed. So when I was at the pharmacy, I bought you some condoms. Your boyfriends are supposed to put these you know w-h-e-r-e.

ACT ONE
Scene 4

EXAMINATION ROOM – A LITTLE WHILE LATER
(Rose holds cotton wool to arm. Blanche is there)

· 203 ·

BLANCHE	Ah, Rose. I wish I knew what to say to make you feel better.
ROSE	Say I'm okay.
BLANCHE	You know, we always tend to think the worst so that when the news does finally come, it's never as bad as we thought it was going to be. *(Doctor enters; Rose eagerly approaches him)*
ROSE	Well?
DOCTOR	Well, the good news is, you appear to be in fine physical shape. Do you have any more questions?
ROSE	Oh-W-Of course. Do I have it?
DOCTOR	Oh, w-we'll have the results when you come back in three days.
ROSE	Three day-? What're you talking about? I expect when I go to a hospital for an AIDS test, to find out.
DOCTOR	I'm sorry, I wish it was faster, but it takes us that long to be sure. I thought you knew.
ROSE	Well I didn't know. First you guys give me that transfusion and now you tell me this.
BLANCHE	Honey, I guess there's not really much you can do.
ROSE	Well, sure there is. There's plenty I can do. Like sit around the house for the next seventy-two hours, scared to death he's going to tell me I have something that's gonna kill me. How am I going to do that, Blanche? How am I going to get through the next three days? *(She runs out of room)*
BLANCHE	Thank you. *(She follows Rose out)* END OF ACT ONE

ACT TWO
Scene 1

KITCHEN – NEXT MORNING
(Dorothy, Sophia and Blanche are there. Dorothy speaks into phone)

DOROTHY   We-What do you mean you're cancelling? . . .
Is there anything I can say to change your
mind? . . . I understand . . . Yeah. Goodbye.
(Hangs up phone)
Swell. Now I don't have a band for the
banquet.

BLANCHE   What happened?

DOROTHY   Oh, they decided to play at the "Free Noriega"
benefit.
(Rose enters, upbeat and hyper)

ROSE   Hi, girls!

BLANCHE   Rose, what were you doing out so early this
morning?

ROSE   Well, I couldn't sleep, so I went for a spin last
night – to Alabama. Blanche, do you know at a
truck stop in Tuscaloosa they have an egg dish
named after you?

BLANCHE   Really? How are they prepared?

SOPHIA   Over easy. Rose, are you okay?

ROSE   I'm fine. Never better. In fact, I'm so fine that
I've decided not to even get my results.

DOROTHY   Oh, now, Rose . . .

ROSE   *(Rose goes to box)*
Oh, look at all this stuff for the celebrity
auction. Linda Evans' compact . . .

DOROTHY   Now, look, Rose . . .

ROSE   Wait, what about the dress Jamie Farr promised us from M*A*S*H?

DOROTHY   No, it hasn't come yet.

ROSE   But he promised.

BLANCHE   Honey, we have a lot of other stuff. It's okay.

ROSE   No, it's not. He let you down. Well-well I'm not surprised. You couldn't trust Klinger on guard duty and you can't trust him now.

DOROTHY   Rose, take it easy.

ROSE   Oh, I'm the one who's supposed to take it easy? Me? When the Klingers of this world are kicking us in the teeth.

DOROTHY   Rose, you're hysterical!

SOPHIA   Wait, I've seen this in the movies.

ROSE   How could he do this? I-What is wrong with the man?
(Sophia slaps Dorothy)

DOROTHY   Ma, you almost got it.

BLANCHE   Listen, I think we're all under a little stress here. Now I have an idea. How about lunch and a movie? My treat.

ROSE   Why not? I still have another fifty-two hours to kill.
(Rose and Blanche exit)

DOROTHY   Oh, this is rough. I feel terrible.

SOPHIA   Yeah, I really feel guilty. Jamie Farr's dress did come. I just remembered where I put it.

DOROTHY   Where?

SOPHIA   How do I look?

ACT TWO
Scene 2

LIVING ROOM – NEXT DAY
(Dorothy is there. Sophia enters from hallway)

DOROTHY	Ma, what were you doing in my bathroom for two hours?
SOPHIA	The hokey-kokey. What do you think I was doing?
DOROTHY	Why were you using my bathroom?
SOPHIA	There's something wrong with mine.
DOROTHY	Oh, what?
SOPHIA	Rose used it.
DOROTHY	Ma, that is just ignorant paranoia.
SOPHIA	Hey, I'm making progress. Yesterday I was using the bathroom down at the Shell station.
DOROTHY	You know, it's attitudes like that that add to the panic about this. Now, what is wrong with you?
SOPHIA	Hey, one little slip and you're all over my back. It won't happen again. Relax. *(Blanche enters)*
BLANCHE	Why is there an "R" on some of our coffee cups? *(Dorothy looks at Sophia)*
SOPHIA	Uh, "R" for regular. Blank ones are decaf.
DOROTHY	I don't believe you!
SOPHIA	Look, I know intellectually there's no way I can catch it. But now that it's so close to home, it's scary.
BLANCHE	Well, Sophia, I'm afraid you're just going to have to get over that.

SOPHIA   I'll try. I'll try. I'm usually not like this. I've
          been using your toothbrush for months.
          (Sophia exits)

ACT TWO
Scene 3

KITCHEN (A WHILE LATER)
(Rose is there. Blanche enters back door)

BLANCHE   Hi, Rose, what's going on?

ROSE   Oh, I'm just sitting here kicking myself for not
          taking care of my gallbladder and for going to
          that hospital for the operation and for letting
          them give me blood without asking first, "Oh,
          excuse me, are you sure this isn't going to kill
          me one day?"

BLANCHE   Now, now, Rose. Take it easy.

ROSE   Why does everyone keep saying that? I don't
          feel like taking it easy. I might have AIDS.
          And it scares the hell out of me. And yet every
          time I open my mouth to talk about it,
          somebody says, "There, there, Rose. Take it
          easy."

BLANCHE   I'm sorry, honey.

ROSE   Why me, Blanche? I'm tired of pretending I feel
          okay so you won't say, "Take it easy". And I'm
          tired of you saying "Take it easy", 'cause you're
          afraid I'm going to fall apart. Damn it, why is
          this happening to me? I mean, this isn't
          supposed to happen to people like me. You
          must have gone to bed with hundreds of men
          and all I had was one innocent operation.
          (Rose storms out to living room)

BLANCHE   Hey! Wait a minute.
           (*Blanche follows her*)
           LIVING ROOM (CONTINUOUS)
           Are you saying this should be me and not you?

ROSE   No. No. I'm just saying that I'm a good person.
           Hell, I'm a goody-two-shoes.

BLANCHE   AIDS is not a bad person's disease, Rose. It is
           not God punishing people for their sins.

ROSE   You're right, Blanche.

BLANCHE   Well, you're damn straight I'm right . . . I'm
           sorry I yelled at you.

ROSE   Oh, don't apologize. I mean, this is what I
           want. I-oh God, this waiting is driving me
           crazy. Blanche, when you were tested how did
           you make it through?

BLANCHE   Just kept it to myself and acted like a real bitch
           to everybody else.

ROSE   No wonder we never knew.
           (*Rose exits*)

ACT TWO
Scene 4

KITCHEN (*A WHILE LATER*)
(*Dorothy, Blanche and Sophia are there. Dorothy pours coffee*)

DOROTHY   These three days are killing Rose.

BLANCHE   What she needs from us are calm heads.

SOPHIA   Then that's what she'll get. Oh God, you gave
           me an "R" cup!

DOROTHY   Ma, will you stop that. Here.
           (*Switches her cup for Sophia's*)

BLANCHE	Listen, we're the only family Rose has here so we have to help her through whatever she's going through.
DOROTHY	Right.
SOPHIA	Sure.
BLANCHE	*(Lifts cup)* So, here's to Rose. Whatever happens, whatever those tests show, we're here for her.
SOPHIA	Dorothy, give me that. *(Dorothy and Sophia exchange cups. The women toast. Sophia drinks from the "R" cup)*

ACT TWO
Scene 5

LANAI – THAT NIGHT
(Rose is lying quietly as Dorothy enters)

DOROTHY	Oh, Rose, excuse me. I didn't know you were out here.
ROSE	It's okay, Dorothy. I was just praying. Trying to put in a good word for tomorrow. What are you doing?
DOROTHY	Ah, just working on this stupid flier for my stupid banquet. It's not important.
ROSE	Sure it is.
DOROTHY	No, it's okay, Rose.
ROSE	No, it is important. What's the matter? *(They move to table)*
DOROTHY	I've rewritten this thing three times and the most persuasive slogan I can come up with is: "Save Our Swamps. No Really, We Mean it."
ROSE	I like it.

DOROTHY   Oh, no you don't.

ROSE   No I don't.

DOROTHY   Sounds like I'm selling *mosquitoes*, Rose. I
           mean, not that they don't serve a purpose. All
           life is precious . . .
           (*Slaps neck with hand*)
           I care about our wetlands, I just wish they were
           more glamorous, you know. I mean, I'm trying
           to save something that you can't go into
           without wearing hip boots.

ROSE   Well, some people might chuckle, but I think
           what you're doing is important. I mean people
           laughed at me back in St. Olaf when I
           spearheaded the drive to get our very own
           missile silo. Oh sure, some Gloomy Gusses
           muttered about the plutonium thing, but I
           figured if we could make our sleepy little hamlet
           into a first strike target, it would help tourism.

DOROTHY   You know, it sounds like we both have a little
           trouble with groups.

ROSE   (*Chuckles*)
           Maybe so.

DOROTHY   You know that in school, I actually joined the
           Math Club so I could meet guys?
           (*Both laugh*)
           Really.

ROSE   Oh, honey. Oh, I can beat that, I joined the
           4-H Club to be hip.
           (*They laugh even harder*)

DOROTHY   (*Points to herself*)
           The Aldo Ray Fan Club.

ROSE   (*Laughs*)
           I can beat that, too.

DOROTHY   Oh, what?

ROSE	No, I can't. That's pretty bad. *(They keep laughing. Dorothy holds Rose's hand)* Ohhh, oh, that felt good. It's been a bad week.
DOROTHY	It'll get better. *(The women smile at each other a beat, then slap their necks)*

ACT TWO
Scene 6

DOCTOR'S OFFICE – NEXT DAY
(The ladies are there. Rose paces. Sophia has newspaper)

ROSE	It's weird. I wanted those three days over. And now that they are, I kind of feel I'd like some of it back. I mean, any second that door is going to open and that doctor's going to tell me my future.
SOPHIA	Your future's going to be filled with nothing but joy and laughter.
ROSE	Thank you, Sophia.
SOPHIA	Don't thank me. Thank the Miami Herald. That's your horoscope. *(Doctor enters)*
DOCTOR	Good morning, ladies.
DOROTHY	Good morning, doctor.
BLANCHE	Good morning.
ROSE	I hope you don't mind, doctor. These are my friends.
DOCTOR	Not at all. Your test results were fine, Mrs. Zbornak.
DOROTHY	Oh, that's great!

ROSE   Well, sure, that's great for you, Dorothy. But what about me?

DOROTHY   Rose, Rose, you used my name. You remember?

ROSE   Right. Well, then I'm, fine, too. I'm fine! Oh, thank you, God.
              (*Then, to doctor*)
              Oh, I wish you could've told me that on the phone. The last couple of hours waiting were the hardest.

DOCTOR   I know, but even people who test negative often need more counselling.

ROSE   Oh, I feel wonderful. I feel great.

DOCTOR   Well, evidently, you had all the emotional support you needed. I know what you've been through. And I'm really very happy things turned out OK.

ROSE   Oh, thank you, doctor.
              (*He exits*)

DOROTHY   Thank you, doctor.

BLANCHE   Hey.

ROSE   Ohhh. Oh. Oh, he's right. You guys were terrific. Thank you for being there for me. And thank you for making me feel you'd always be there for me – no matter what happened.

BLANCHE   Bet you'd like to go home now and get some rest.

ROSE   No. No I haven't felt like I've been living for three days. I want to go with you to the fund-raiser.

DOROTHY   Great. And it's going to be a success. You know Ma must have stuffed and mailed over five hundred invitations.

(Rose, Blanche and Dorothy exit)

SOPHIA Stuffed?

END OF ACT TWO

CHEATERS

Written by: TOM WHEDON
Directed by: TERRY HUGHES

· *Introduction* ·

IT SEEMS THAT NO Golden Girl is ever too old to feel like a silly schoolgirl. In an episode which homes in on trust and self-respect, Dorothy is about to fall in love with ex-boyfriend, Glen, whom she finally suspects of being a lifelong cheater, while Sophia and Blanche are conned out of a sizeable sum at the shopping mall.

Dorothy, having had an affair with married Glen four years before, receives a call from him and, insisting that "he was trapped in a bad marriage", is faced with her mother's stony, but always amusing, realism.

Sophia: "There's no such thing as being 'trapped' in a marriage. In this country you can get divorced. In Sicily there was no divorce. If you wanted to end a marriage, we had to resort to the 'lupara'."

Rose: "Is that some kind of legal loophole?"

Sophia: "It's some kind of sawed-off shotgun."

To highlight the gravity which Dorothy attaches to her involvement with Glen, Blanche breezes in to announce yet another night spent in an hotel room with one Mel Bushman, though this time indulging in "one of our 'where is this relationship going' talks." Unfortunately for Blanche, sex was not invited into the room: "God, if only he didn't want to talk."

It is Rose who, despite being stamped on by Blanche as a loser for her insistence on self-respect, tries to steer Dorothy on the sensible track away from Glen. Yet Dorothy, keen to reinvigorate her time with Glen, falls in with Blanche in the first instance.

Rose: "Well sure y-you'll have some great times and fabulous sex but is that worth your self-respect?"

Dorothy: "Not now, loser."

Despite Sophia's old-fashioned warning that Glen is an adulterer and that Dorothy should "keep both feet on the floor", Dorothy goes ahead anyway, only to eventually realise that Glen is primarily afraid of being alone. Glen, meanwhile, has charmed Sophia into next week, and, wondering if her daughter will resemble her in thirty years time is told flatly by Dorothy, "only if you lock me in the dryer."

In an episode where Dorothy's relaxed common sense gives way to girlish spontaneity, and Rose's airhead ideas give way to common sense, Sophia's streetwise sharpness is elbowed by a sting at the shopping mall. Both Sophia and Blanche are duped by a seemingly decent man, a fake nun and a shaggy-dog tale of a bulging wallet. In spite of their mutual worldliness, both ladies are easily taken in.

It is the now sensible Rose who prompts them to inform the police of the sting:

"The reason these confidence men don't get caught is because people are embarrassed to come forward and admit they were conned."

Taking her sound advice, Blanche drops an amusing line in to the mix which typifies the wonderfully surreal Jewish twist at the heart of American television humour:

"They want us to come down tomorrow and pick out nuns from a lineup."

CAST

DOROTHY, ROSE, BLANCHE, SOPHIA, GLEN, KANE, NUN

ACT ONE

Scene 1

KITCHEN – Morning
(Sophia at stove. Dorothy pours coffee, sits. Rose enters)

ROSE   Morning.

DOROTHY   Oh, morning, honey.

ROSE   I had the strangest dream last night. I was at a baseball game. Charlie Brown was pitching and Shroeder was behind the plate and Lucy and Snoopy were in the outfield. And they wouldn't let me play. When I woke up I was crying. What do you suppose it all means?

DOROTHY   Peanuts Envy?
(Blanche enters)

BLANCHE   Good morning.

DOROTHY   Oh, m-hey, you got home pretty late last night. When I went to bed you still weren't in.

BLANCHE   Well, I was up all night with Mel Bushman having one of our "where is this relationship going" talks.

DOROTHY   Oh? And where is it going?

BLANCHE   Where it usually goes. Room 506 at the Quality Court. Ohhh, I hate him. God, if only he didn't want to talk. Oh, by the way – right after I got in you got a phone call. Uh, from a Glen somebody.

DOROTHY   Glen O'Brien?

BLANCHE   Uh-huh.

DOROTHY   Di-Did he leave a number?

ROSE   Who's Glen O'Brien?

SOPHIA   He's the married guy she shacked up with four years ago.

DOROTHY   And look, I'm not proud of what I did, but it didn't seem so bad at the time. He was trapped in a bad marriage.

SOPHIA   There's no such thing as being "trapped" in a marriage. In this country you can get divorced. In Sicily there was no divorce. If you wanted to end a marriage, we had to resort to the "lupara".

ROSE   Is that some kind of legal loophole?

SOPHIA   It's some kind of sawed-off shotgun.

DOROTHY   Blanche, did he leave a number?

BLANCHE   No.

SOPHIA   Dorothy, dropping him was the smartest thing you ever did.

ROSE   What are you going to do if he calls again?

SOPHIA   Don't talk to him.

BLANCHE   Oh, why not? Four years is a long time. Maybe he's divorced.

DOROTHY   What, you think?

BLANCHE   Well sure. Why else would he call?

ROSE   Oh-stay away from him.

BLANCHE   Oh, see him.

ROSE   Keep some self-respect.

BLANCHE   Self-respect is for losers like Rose.

ROSE Well sure y-you'll have some great times and some fabulous sex, but is that worth your self-respect?

DOROTHY Not now, loser.
(*Dorothy exits*)

ACT ONE
Scene 2

LIVING ROOM – LATER THAT MORNING
(*Dorothy sits by phone*)
PHONE RINGS
(*Dorothy gets it*)

DOROTHY Hello? . . .
(*Listens*)
Oh, l-look, I'm-I'm sorry I'm going to have to interrupt. No, I-I'm sure this is a very worthy cause, but, uh, no, to be perfectly frank, at this moment I couldn't give a flying fig about whooping cranes. No, no, I have to keep the line free . . . Uh, yuh-Fine, I'll send a check. Uh, hold it, let me grab a pencil.
(*Writes in air*)
Okay. Whopping Cranes, yuh, Box 1990, Newcastle, Louisiana. Got it. Glad I could help. Bye-Bye.
(*Hangs up. Sophia and Blanche enter from hallway*)

SOPHIA Hey, Dorothy! Blanche is taking me to the mall. You wanna come?

DOROTHY I don't think so, Ma.

BLANCHE Oh, honey, come on. You're not teaching today. It'll be fun.

DOROTHY No, I think I'd just rather sit here and read.

PHONE RINGS
(Dorothy gets it)
Hello? . . . Oh, hi. Yes, I heard you called.
What a pleasant surprise . . . We-uh, I-oo-I-I'm
pretty sure I can make it. Just let me check my
book.
(Dorothy waits a few beats)
I seem to be clear.

SOPHIA   *(To Blanche)*
He must have asked her out this century.

DOROTHY   Where? . . . Fine, fine. All right . . . Bye-bye.
(Hangs up phone)

BLANCHE   What did he say?

DOROTHY   W-He said that he has something important he
wants to talk about.

BLANCHE   Oh, that's my favourite lie.

SOPHIA   Dorothy, you'll be sorry.

DOROTHY   Oh, Ma, come on, we liked each other. He's a
funny, warm, giving man. He made me laugh. I
am seeing him.

SOPHIA   All right. Go ahead. Meet your adulterer. But
remember, you were brought up a lady. Keep
both your feet on the floor.

DOROTHY   I'd better go change.
(To Blanche)
Blanche, what should I wear?

BLANCHE   Well, if you're gonna keep both feet on the
floor, something you can pull off over your
head.

ACT ONE
Scene 3

MALL – LATER THAT DAY
(Blanche and Sophia are seated with drinks)

SOPHIA   I don't care what that salesgirl said. I looked good in that bathing suit. You know, sometimes I wish I did live in Brazil.
(They sit a moment. Kane approaches)

KANE   *(Shows wallet)* Excuse me – one of you ladies drop this?

SOPHIA   Is there money in it?

KANE   *(Examining it)*
Uh-huh.

SOPHIA   I dropped it.

KANE   *(Simultaneous with Blanche's speech below)*
There's a lot of money . . .

BLANCHE   Sophia! You did nothing of the kind!

KANE   There's a lot of money in here.

BLANCHE   That does look a little bit like Sophia's wallet.

KANE   It's a man's wallet. Now, did either of you see who did drop it?

BLANCHE   'Fraid not. No.

KANE   There's over two thousand dollars in here. Whoever lost this must be frantic. I think we should turn it in to the Lost & Found.

SOPHIA   Wait a minute? You're going to give that kind of money to a guy who makes two bucks an hour watching umbrellas?

KANE   That's a good point. Besides, there's no I.D. in here. Now, what if we put a notice in the newspaper. And after a certain amount of time if-if nobody claimed the wallet, then we could –

BLANCHE   Split it. Then we could split it. I know that is what I would want people to do if *I* lost *my* wallet.

KANE   Sure.

SOPHIA   Hold it. In the meantime, who's gonna keep the money?
(To Kane)
I don't know you enough to trust you. And her I know –
(Indicating Blanche)
– so we got a problem.

KANE   Now, this is off-the-top-of-my-head stuff, but maybe we're too close to the problem. Maybe we should ask somebody who doesn't have a stake in this and maybe they could find a solution. Dumb idea?

BLANCHE   Well, it's worth a try.
(They look around, spot nun shopping)

KANE   How about that nun over there?

SOPHIA   What if she guilts us into giving it to charity?

KANE   Well, I think we can agree that that's the last thing we want to do.

BLANCHE   On the other hand, she is a shopping nun. She could be okay.
(Kane approaches nun)

KANE   Excuse me? Sister?

NUN   Yes?
(Sophia and Blanche join them)

KANE   Um, these ladies and I found a wallet with some money in it.

BLANCHE   Yes, but until the rightful owner shows up to claim it, we were wondering where we could put it so it'd be safe?

NUN   In a bank?

SOPHIA   But whose bank?

NUN   Well, couldn't you open up a joint account, in all your names?

KANE   Um, I don't know. See, I-I really don't know these people.

NUN   Oh, well, maybe you could both put up equal amounts of your own money to show mutual good faith and open up an account. And if the money isn't claimed, then you could withdraw it all and split it. And if it is, well, at least you've made some interest.

BLANCHE   Oh, that sounds too complicated.

KANE   I think it would work. I-I'd certainly be willing to put up two thousand dollars of my money if you two would put up a thousand each.
(*To nun*)
Thank you so much for your help, Sister.

NUN   Yes. Go with God.
(*She crosses away*)

BLANCHE   Sophia, I just don't know.

SOPHIA   Oh, c'mon, Dorothy's bank is right over there. She lets me draw on her account. If he's honest enough to put up his money, we should be willing to do the same.

BLANCHE   I guess it seems fair, okay.

KANE   Great. Let's go.
(*They start to leave*)

BLANCHE   Now, Sophia, remember, found money is

supposed to be spent on something frivolous, something you would never buy for yourself.

SOPHIA   What are you going to get, underwear?
           (*They exit. Nun watches them go, lights cigarette*)

ACT ONE
Scene 4

GLEN'S APARTMENT – LATER THAT DAY
(*Glen is there*)

DOORBELL
(*He opens door. It's Dorothy*)

GLEN   Dorothy.

DOROTHY   Hi.

GLEN   You look very pretty.

DOROTHY   So do you.

GLEN   Come in.

DOROTHY   Mmm. Nice place.

GLEN   Yeah, well, I was left a little strapped by the settlement. Can I get you something to drink?

DOROTHY   Settlement?

GLEN   The divorce settlement. Y-I got to keep half my self-respect and she got to keep everything else. Anyway, that's why I had to talk to you. I had to find out . . . how you were doing.

DOROTHY   Oh, I'm fine. I'm fine. I'm doing just fine. Maybe I will have just a glass of water.
           (*He gets it for her*)
           Gee, it seems so strange not meeting you in a hotel room. I guess I shouldn't steal the towels.

GLEN   Ooh, towels. Yeah, I gotta put that on my

shopping list.
(*Writes on list*)
Right next to soap . . . and broad with job.
(*They laugh*)
I've missed you, Dorothy.

DOROTHY   (*He gives her water. She sips. He sits*)
Mm. Good water. Yeah-I'm having a little
trouble getting used to the idea that, uh, you're
divorced because I remember you told me that,
uh, no matter how bad the marriage was, you
felt that you were too old to just leave it for an
uncertain future.

GLEN   Kidding. No, ah, actually, I didn't have any
choice in the matter; she divorced *me*.

DOROTHY   Oh? What-what happened? She found you with
someone else?

GLEN   No, she found herself with someone else. Uh, I
can't say that I blame her. I mean, there was
really nothing left between us. Listen, since
things are different now, you think there's any
chance that we could start over?

DOROTHY   Oh, w-I don't know. You know, uh, four years
. . .

GLEN   Is there someone else?

DOROTHY   No. No, there's no one else.

GLEN   Good.
(*Moves closer to her*)

DOROTHY   Um, y-y-you know what's interesting? I, um, I
just read somewhere that, uh, the cells in the
human body, uh, completely regenerate
themselves every, w-uh, seven years. Isn't that,
uh, interesting?

GLEN   (*Takes her glass, sets it on table*)
Uh-huh.

DOROTHY I, I-g-I guess that means that we're, uh, forty
         percent of, uh, who we were, uh, you know,
         four, uh, years ago.

GLEN   Dorothy.

DOROTHY Yes?
         (He kisses her)

DOROTHY Actually, it's four and a half years. So, uh, that
         makes it closer to thirty-five percent. You know
         what? The last thing my mother said to me was
         that she wanted me to keep my feet on the
         floor.

GLEN   My mother wanted me to be a priest.

DOROTHY I guess it's a bad day for mothers.
         (They head for the bedroom)
         END OF ACT ONE

ACT TWO
Scene 1

LIVING ROOM – LATER THAT DAY
*(Rose is seated, doing crossword. Blanche and Sophia come in
front door. They seem surprised to see Rose, and secretive)*

BLANCHE Rose!

ROSE   Hi. How did shopping go?

SOPHIA   Great. Great. It was great.

BLANCHE Really great. Best shopping ever.

ROSE   I was just gonna make some lemonade. I'll bet
         your girls could really use some.

BLANCHE/ Great.
SOPHIA

ROSE   *(Gets up)*
         Okeydokey.

(*She exits to kitchen, they watch her go*)

BLANCHE   Sophia, remember we swore. We don't tell anybody.

SOPHIA   Not even Dorothy? I think I owe it to her. It was her money.

BLANCHE   Nobody. I just couldn't stand the humiliation. You want the world to know that a perfect stranger tricked us out of two thousand dollars!?

SOPHIA   Okay, okay. I won't tell anybody. You don't have to worry about me, Blanche. No one'll get a word out of me. I swear on my Uncle Guido's grave.

ACT TWO
Scene 2

KITCHEN – LATER THAT AFTERNOON
(*Sophia and Rose at table*)

SOPHIA   . . . Then the guy gave us the envelope with his money, our money and the found money in it. Blanche and I went to open the joint account and when the teller opened the envelope, there were just scraps of paper in it.
(*Blanche enters from living room*)
I don't remember any more. That's all you're going to get from me no matter how many times you hit me.

BLANCHE   Sophia! What about your Uncle Guido?!

SOPHIA   He's fine. I got a postcard from him this morning.

ROSE   You two were victims of the oldest confidence game going: the pigeon drop.

BLANCHE   But he just seemed so honest.

ROSE   Well, that's why it's called a confidence game. I
            mean, he has to win your confidence or you
            wouldn't put up the money.

SOPHIA   It wasn't his idea – the nun suggested it.

ROSE   She was part of the team. They always work in
            pairs.

SOPHIA   I don't know what the Church is coming to. I
            thought it stopped with bingo.

ROSE   That was no nun. I work for a consumer
            protection show. We've been warning people
            about this for months. Once these scamsters
            have your money in an envelope, they make a
            switch and you wind up with worthless paper.
            They prey on the old and gullible.

BLANCHE   Are you calling me gullible?

ROSE   No.

BLANCHE   Oh. Uh.

ROSE   There is one thing I think you should both do
            right away in-inform the police.

BLANCHE   Oh, forget it.

ROSE   The reason these confidence men don't get
            caught is because people are embarrassed to
            come forward and admit they were conned.

BLANCHE   I'm sorry, Rose, I just can't.

ROSE   Well, perhaps this little story might make you
            change your mind. Back in St. Olaf there was
            this shepherd boy who tended his flock on the
            hill above the town. A wolf kept coming down
            and stealing his sheep, but the boy never
            caught him doing it. Because he never saw it
            happening, he became known around St. Olaf
            as "The boy who didn't cry 'wolf'.' Anyway,
            one day the townspeople heard the boy on the

hill yelling, "Wolf! Wolf!" Well, they all figured if the boy never cried "wolf" when the wolf *was* there, if he yelled "wolf" now, it stood to reason the wolf *wasn't* there.

SOPHIA   Boy, nothing gets by your people.

ROSE   Damn straight. It was a bear; a huge, ferocious grizzly bear.

SOPHIA   What happened to the boy?

ROSE   He became known as "the boy who cried continuously".

ACT TWO
Scene 3

LIVING ROOM – AFTERNOON (A FEW DAYS LATER)
(Sophia is there. Rose is there. Blanche enters)

BLANCHE   I just got off the phone with a Sergeant Delfino of the Bunco Squad. He said they picked up two people who matched the description we gave them. They want us to come down tomorrow and pick out nuns from a lineup.

ROSE   That must make you feel proud.

BLANCHE   Well now, that's what Sergeant Delfino said: "Why you must feel proud knowing that by having come forth as you have, you have possibly saved other oldsters from a similar rip-off." He called me an "oldster"! I called him a "pig". We're having dinner on Saturday.

ACT TWO
Scene 4

PORCH – AFTERNOON (CONTINUOUS)
(Dorothy and Glen approach front door. Glen holds pastry box)

DOROTHY	I really appreciate this, your meeting my mother.
GLEN	Hey, you want to get married?
DOROTHY	You mean instead of meeting my mother?
GLEN	No, we can do both.
DOROTHY	This is kind of sudden.
GLEN	Well, think about it.
DOROTHY	I will. I mean, this is something to think about.
GLEN	Okay, let's go.
DOROTHY	Oh God this is gonna be awful.
GLEN	I'm looking forward to this. I mean, you meet the mother, it gives you a pretty good idea what the daughter's gonna look like in thirty years.
DOROTHY	Only if you lock me in the dryer. *(Dorothy straightens and opens door)*

ACT TWO
Scene 5

LIVING ROOM (CONTINUOUS)
(Dorothy and Glen enter. Sophia, Blanche and Rose are there)

DOROTHY	Everybody, this is Glen. Glen, I'd like you to meet . . .
GLEN	Nope, don't tell me . . . *(Identifying them correctly)* . . . Rose . . . Blanche . . . and Mrs. Petrillo . . . *(Hands Sophia pastry box)* These are for you.
SOPHIA	*(Opening it)* Cannoli! What does an Irishman know about cannoli?

GLEN   Hey, when I was a kid in Brooklyn every
        Sunday my father used to go to Zampano's
        Bakery for cannoli.

DOROTHY *(To Glen)*
        I never dreamed you grew up in Brooklyn.

GLEN   Oh sure. Our whole block was Irish, the other
        block was Italian. We used to take turns
        beating each other up on the way home from
        school.

ROSE   I think it's nice when kids take turns.

DOROTHY Yeah. Uh, Blanche, honey, could I see you in
        the kitchen for a minute?

BLANCHE Oh sure.

DOROTHY Yeah. I'll be right back, Glen. I think you'll be
        okay.
        (Dorothy and Blanche start for kitchen)

SOPHIA So, Glen, how come you cheated on your wife?
        (Dorothy shoots her a look)

GLEN   Wow. Straight to Final Jeopardy, huh? Okay,
        Bernice and I had been separated emotionally
        for years when I met Dorothy. And right or
        wrong, I've never been anything but grateful
        that that happened. What else you want to
        know about me?

BLANCHE Sophia, I think it's time you stopped subjecting
        this nice man to the third degree.

SOPHIA I had to check him out. Dorothy's a smart,
        attractive girl, but when it comes to picking
        men, she's all thumbs. But she's clean and she's
        got good teeth . . .
        (Offers him Cannoli)
        Cannoli?
        (Dorothy and Blanche exit to kitchen)

ACT TWO
Scene 6

KITCHEN (CONTINUOUS)
(Dorothy and Blanche enter)

DOROTHY   I had to tell somebody and I couldn't wait another minute. Glen asked me to marry him!

BLANCHE   Pay dirt!
(Then)
Well, are you gonna do it?

DOROTHY   I . . .I haven't had time to make up my mind.

BLANCHE   Honey, don't dawdle. Now, men have a very short memory span when it comes to that question. Sometimes they forget before you can get your clothes back on.
(Rose enters)

ROSE   Oh, Dorothy, Glen is such a charmer. He and Sophia are really getting along.

BLANCHE   *(To Dorothy)*
Can I tell her?
(Dorothy nods)
Glen asked Dorothy to marry him.

ROSE   Do it! Oh, marry him, Dorothy. Even if you have to sign one of those prenatal agreements.

DOROTHY   Oh, I'm so happy. Am I too happy? Oh, I, why am I so happy? Is this too good to be true?

BLANCHE   You are such a pessimist, always looking on the dark side.

DOROTHY   Oh, well a fine pessimist I'd be if I didn't. Oh, girls, group hug!

BLANCHE   Oh, Dorothy, Oh, Dorothy.

ROSE   Oh, oh.
(They all laugh and embrace)

ACT TWO
Scene 7

Kitchen – That Night
(Sophia is there. Dorothy enters)

DOROTHY   Ma, what are you doing up?

SOPHIA   Aw, just having a Maalox moment. What about you?

DOROTHY   Oh, thinking about Glen. Oh, this whole thing is so rushed. Ma, I'm afraid. I'm too old to make another mistake. I don't want to make a fool out of myself.

SOPHIA   Pussycat, you're never too old to make a fool of yourself. Those were your exact words when I told you I lost that money. And you were right. I never felt so stupid. 'Course, I would've felt a lot more stupid if it'd been my money instead of yours.

DOROTHY   Ma, what do you think I should do?

SOPHIA   Nobody can help you with that decision, Dorothy. I can't tell you what to do. I mean, I won't be around forever. I'd like to know there was someone here to love you and take care of you like you take care of me. Maybe he could give you a bigger allowance. I mean, it's nice now and then to buy something that's not generic. You know what I'm saying, Dorothy?

DOROTHY   Yes, Ma. And it's nice. You're saying you love me and you care.

SOPHIA   No, I'm saying buy genuine Q-tips. If I'm gonna put a stick in my ear, I'd like a little cotton at the end.
(She exits)

ACT TWO
Scene 8

GLEN'S APARTMENT – NEXT DAY
(Glen and Dorothy enter)

GLEN   Oh, remind me before you leave. I went back to the bakery and got your mother some anise cookies.

DOROTHY   You don't have to try so hard. You know, to be honest I still can't believe how much my mother liked you.

GLEN   Yeah, I liked her, too. One thing puzzled me, though. When you were all in the kitchen, why did she keep asking me if I'd lost this wallet with fifty bucks in it?

DOROTHY   My mom, the eternal Girl Scout.

GLEN   You were very quiet on the way over.

DOROTHY   You gave me a lot to think about.

GLEN   Aw, come on, you had to see it coming.

DOROTHY   I just didn't expect it so soon.

GLEN   So what do you say? Marry me and take me away from all this.
PHONE RINGS
Excuse me.
(Gets it)
Hello . . . Oh hello, Bernice . . . No, I'm alone. Well, what do you want? . . . Yeah, sure, I'll sign them tomorrow . . . Okay. 'Bye.
(Hangs up)

DOROTHY   "I'm alone"?

GLEN   It's . . . it's gonna take awhile for everybody to get used to this. So, what do you say? Will you marry me? I wanna get my life together, I mean, I'm . . . I'm really no good being single. Ju . . . just look around.

DOROTHY I am . . . looking and listening and I can't help but remember that um, I've been in the room before when your wife called and you said you were alone. Then you were cheating on her.

GLEN With you.

DOROTHY Yes, but I've also been Bernice and had my husband call me. And he was always alone, too. You know, I was married to Stanley for thirty-eight years and for approximately thirty-nine of those years he cheated on me.

GLEN I told a little lie because it's gonna take her some time to get used to the idea of you and me.

DOROTHY Yeah, well, I'm going to need a little time to get used to it, too. Look, I'm . . .I'm not saying you're a cheater. I'm not saying that . . .that you're like Stan. I don't know, maybe there's something wrong with me, that I'm . . .I'm not trusting enough. But, uh, I'm gonna need some time.

GLEN So what are you telling me? It's gonna be months or years? Or maybe never? Dorothy, if we were both twenty-five, I could wait. But I need someone in my life now.

DOROTHY Are you sure that you want to marry me or, or are you just afraid to be alone?

GLEN Who wants to be alone?

DOROTHY Nobody. I don't. But if you're marrying me because I happen to be on the top of the list then, uh, maybe I shouldn't be on the list.
(After a beat)

GLEN	So, I guess this is it, huh?
DOROTHY	I guess so.
GLEN	I still love you, Dorothy.
DOROTHY	I love you, too.
GLEN	If you change your mind . . .
DOROTHY	If you change yours . . . *(Smiles and she exits. A beat. She re-enters)* There's no reason why my mother shouldn't have the cookies. *(She takes them and exits. Glen looks around his now empty apartment)* END OF ACT TWO